WRITE COPY, MAKE MONEY

ANDY MASLEN

WRITE COPY, MAKE MONEY

HOW TO BUILD YOUR OWN SUCCESSFUL FREELANCE COPYWRITING BUSINESS

Marshall Cavendish
Business

Copyright © 2011 Andy Maslen

First published in 2011 by Marshall Cavendish Business
An imprint of Marshall Cavendish International

PO Box 65829
London EC1P 1NY
United Kingdom

and

1 New Industrial Road
Singapore 536196
genrefsales@sg.marshallcavendish.com
www.marshallcavendish.com/genref

Marshall Cavendish is a trademark of Times Publishing Limited

Other Marshall Cavendish offices:
Marshall Cavendish International (Asia) Private Limited, 1 New Industrial Road, Singapore 536196 • Marshall Cavendish Corporation. 99 White Plains Road, Tarrytown NY 10591–9001, USA • Marshall Cavendish International (Thailand) Co Ltd. 253 Asoke, 12th Floor, Sukhumvit 21 Road, Klongtoey Nua, Wattana, Bangkok 10110, Thailand • Marshall Cavendish (Malaysia) Sdn Bhd, Times Subang, Lot 46, Subang Hi-Tech Industrial Park, Batu Tiga, 40000 Shah Alam, Selangor Darul Ehsan, Malaysia

A CIP record for this book is available from the British Library

ISBN 978-981-4302-58-6

Cover design by OpalWorks Pte Ltd

Printed and bound in United Kingdom by TJ International Ltd

To the two guys who eased my transition from the corporate world and helped me find true happiness as a freelance copywriter.

Contents

Acknowledgements

Once again, I would like to thank our clients. Without them I wouldn't have much to talk about on the subject of freelance copywriting.

The second group of people I want to thank are the 16 freelance copywriters who generously gave their time, and shared their wisdom, in the interviews in Section Nine. Without their contributions this book would be a far less interesting read. They are: Tom Albrighton (ABC Copywriting); Matt Ambrose (CopywritersCrucible); Relly Annett-Baker (PoppyCopy); Caroline Gibson; Caroline Hampstead; Richard Harrison (RichWords); Anthony Hewson (AH copy); Jane Kingsmill (KingsmillInk); Vince Love (Write Concepts); Claire McCarthy (thetopcopy); Abbe Opher; Sally Ormond (Briar Copywriting); Jill Tomlinson (Jill Tomlinson Copywriting); Johnny Thomson (Thomson Media); Sarah Turner (TurnerInk); and Peter Wise (IdeasWise).

The other freelance copywriter I want to thank, but whom I didn't formally interview for this book, is Jo Kelly. She and I started Sunfish in 1996; her experience in marketing and sales and her skills as a writer have helped us build Sunfish into the agency it is today. She also read the manuscript and helped me iron out a few wrinkles.

I'd also like to thank my friends Sally Bibb and Ross Speirs. Sal took time out from her incredibly busy schedule to read the manuscript in its early form and offer constructive advice on how to discuss the occasional ethical challenges freelancers have to face. Ross has always been an inspiring example of how to run your own business and have fun at the same time – he has taught me much about riding out the peaks and troughs. I would also like to thank Martin Liu at Marshall Cavendish for his support and enthusiasm every time I pitch a book idea to him.

Lastly, a huge thank you to my family. You make it all worthwhile.

Foreword

I wish to God I had had this book when I started writing for a living over 50 years ago.

It would probably have doubled my income and halved my pain.

It is full of wise, practical advice:

- On how to organise yourself and your time – two things most writers are astoundingly bad at.

- On how to deal with clients (and prevent them driving you mad).

- On what to charge – with some revealing and helpful figures.

- On having the right attitude when, for example, people want to tamper with your matchless prose.

Somebody once remarked that whenever two writers meet, they always talk about money.

No wonder. Most business people write every day – and think they do it well.

So paying someone else to do it comes very hard. And if you happen to be the someone else, making a good living is damn hard.

This will make it far, far easier.

There are many (too many!) books on how to write better stuff.

But nothing I have seen on how to manage your writing business well.

And nobody I know is better suited to tell you what you need to know, because Andy Maslen has an enviable combination of abilities: he writes well, and he is businesslike.

A good investment in your future.

Drayton Bird

Introduction

On Friday, 13 November 1996, I was a 34-year-old marketing director of an international research publisher. I had a company car, a good salary and bonus, health insurance, paid holidays, a company pension scheme, an office in central London and high status within my company and the industry in which we operated. But everything was about to change.

I came back from a holiday to find that my department had been reorganised from under me. It seems the people who owned the business had realised something: I just wasn't cut out to be a marketing director. I don't blame them; I really wasn't very good at the job. Here's what had happened.

They'd promoted me from marketing assistant to marketing executive because I was a good copywriter and could bring in sales. Ditto from marketing executive to marketing manager. But now I was expected to spend most of my time managing other people. Because I had a good team, that arrangement worked and so, inevitably, I was promoted again. Now we had the company's best copywriter (no false modesty here) doing no copywriting, but expected to produce sales forecasts, spreadsheets, management reports and all the rest. It turns out that sneaking off to write copy when you should be discussing budgets is frowned upon. And rightly so I suppose.

After much wailing and gnashing of teeth, I left.

On Monday, 16 November, 1996, all my executive trappings were behind me. I had nothing. Well, OK, not nothing precisely. I had a PC, a printer and a telephone in the tiny back bedroom of our flat in West London and a fistful of business cards from my contacts. (Oh, and an agreement to work three days a week for my former employers – very helpful when you're starting out.) This book draws on my experience as an independent copywriter in the years since then. It's full of practical lessons that I have learned the hard way and which I hope you can learn the easy way.

You may already have an established copywriting business. Or you might be considering a move into freelancing. Either way, good luck and keep that freelance flag flying.

Andy Maslen
Salisbury 2010

SECTION 1
TAKING THE PLUNGE

Happily for us, copywriting is tailor-made for being outsourced.

Copy is everywhere. Press ads, emails, websites, posters, AdWords, mailshots, bus-sides, advertorials, press releases: they're all stuffed with words. That means copy. And that means copywriters. There are four groups of people who write that copy. In-house marketing people, who *might* be doing a good job, depending on their talents. Non-marketing people, often general managers, business owners or PAs ... who *could* be doing a good job, but it's unlikely, given all the other things they have to deal with. Agency copywriters, who ought to be doing a good job. And freelancers.

The demand for copy

There's a huge and increasing demand for copy. When I started my career, the web didn't exist. So although there was a good deal of advertising and direct marketing, there simply wasn't a market for web copywriting, email copywriting or any other copy for digital media. Economic trends are also playing their part. The number of internet entrepreneurs is spiralling upwards, and there are more start-ups than ever before. And they all have websites, they all need press releases, brochures, case studies, blogs and ... and ...and...

This is good news for you and me. We belong in that fourth category. Or want to. You may be a marketing manager right now, but wishing you had more control over your career, or more time to spend copywriting; or an agency copywriter who fancies running your own business. Or you may have already made the move – recently or in the dim and distant. The work is there. The money is there. The fun, praise and fulfilment are there – if you know where to look, how to get the work, and how to do it.

Learning your trade

Although this isn't a book about copywriting itself, it's worth spending a few paragraphs on the subject. To be a successful freelance copywriter, you are going to have to learn your trade. You are going to have to be able to write copy better than your clients could produce. Given that they are incredibly busy running a department, an agency or a company, that won't be too difficult. Here are my recommendations…

Read all the books you can get your hands on about advertising, marketing, selling skills and copywriting. There are lots to choose from. The authors on my shelves include: Drayton Bird, Robert Bly, James Borg, John Caples, Robert Cialdini, John Fraser-Robinson, Claude Hopkins, Graeme McCorkell, David Ogilvy, Victor Schwab, Joseph Sugarman, Nick Usborne, Joe Vitale and Walter Weintz.

Read blogs, e-zines and e-books – but remember to engage your critical faculties first. The difference between a book and a blog is that the former only comes into existence because an independent authority – a publisher – has invested a lot of time and money in bringing it to market. That's a reasonable guarantee of quality, and of the reliability of the author. (I confess to an interest here – I have published three other books on copywriting with Marshall Cavendish. It's still true though.)

Read copy with a professional eye. Look around you. As I said right at the beginning of this section, copy is everywhere. Never again bin a mailshot without reading it first. Don't flick past the ads in your favourite magazine or newspaper – analyse them and try to determine what the writer was trying to achieve. And whether or not they did. Read web copy and HTML e-mails thoroughly and look for evidence of keyword use, hypertext and usability.

Invest in some training. There are lots of copywriting courses to choose from, some organised by the freelance copywriters

To be a successful freelance copywriter, you are going to have to learn your trade. You are going to have to be able to write copy better than your clients could produce.

interviewed in this book. Some by me. You will pick up new tricks and meet your fellow freelancers.

And, of course, practise. If you're established already, that's easy. If you're building up your business, spend time every day writing copy. Not just blog posts either – I mean selling copy. Treat it as an apprenticeship – copy out direct mail letters or websites you find referenced in books. Write different versions of ads, websites or leaflets you come across.

Why freelance works

Organisations are frequently willing to hire a freelance to write their copy.

Happily for us, copywriting is tailor-made for being outsourced. It's a learnable skill, it's to some extent a technical skill, but it doesn't, for most organisations, have any great strategic value. Unlike general management, R&D, knowledge management or strategy itself, which do, for example. That means organisations are frequently willing to hire a freelance to write their copy. Think of yourself as an intellectual technician – as a Canadian small business guru called me once – and you won't be too far off the mark. Or a plumber, if "intellectual" feels a bit fancy-pants for you.

When I started out on my own, I had originally intended – or imagined, at least – that I would be working for the most part as a freelance marketing director. I would go into companies, diagnose problems, and then offer recommendations for putting them right. A marketing consultant, in other words. What actually happened, reflecting my own interests, was that I would usually focus on the copywriting, which was uniformly off the pace, and suggest that this, above all, was what needed sorting out. "Well can you do it then?" was what my early clients usually asked. And me being me, I always said "Of course." Very quickly I realised that it was far easier to sell copywriting than consultancy. To agree they need the latter service, clients had to make a bigger decision – that they needed help running their own business (or a part of it) more effectively. Nobody needs to admit to anything of the sort to hire a copywriter. They can just say "We're not specialists and we're too busy". Bingo!

Furthermore, the market is very well established. Contrary to what a lot of freelance copywriters seem to think, judging from the copy on their own websites, you don't need to explain to your clients why they should use a professional copywriter. Not if you want clients who pay well and aren't always quibbling because "I could have written that". Clients Googling for freelance copywriters already know that it's better to go outside. Otherwise why are they doing it?

No more nine-to-five

As a freelance copywriter you do have that joyous moment when you realise millions of people are struggling in to work through traffic or on crowded trains and you're snug in your home office or sublet space in a firm of local designers. No commute. No "jacket on the chair" syndrome. No unpaid overtime. Or not if you get your pricing right – of which more in Section 5.

You do have to be disciplined though. People often say to me, "Don't you find it hard to work at home?" They mean with all the distractions on offer, from daytime TV to a garden crying out for some TLC. They are thinking of the times when they "work" from home – "work" in this phrase being a synonym for checking emails while watching telly. My answer is always the same: "I don't find it hard to be disciplined at all. If I don't work, I don't make any money. And if I promise a client I'll deliver the first draft by Friday at 10.00 am, that's what I have to do." So your discipline, and mine, means planning your day or your week or your month so you get the work done AND fit in those other things, which could well be daytime TV or playing on your games console, childcare, shopping, making harpsichords in your garage, or anything else you fancy. Just remember this simple three-word mantra...

Clients come first.

Clients come first.

Clients come first.

Clients come first.

Clients come first.

It can help to chant it over a CD of whale music.

Achieving work/life balance

I have never been entirely comfortable with the "work/life" balance thing. Even though I once wrote a website for someone whose whole consultancy business operated on that very premise. It implies, to me at least, that there is something called work and there's something else called life and you have to balance the two. Yes, of course I know what they're driving at because for many people work takes over their lives. But to be specific, I think what we're really talking about is work/non-work balance. Or what used to be summed up in the saying, "All work and no play makes Jack a dull boy". And, possibly, one needing counselling, anti-depressants, and a hobby or two.

We need to make sure our work doesn't take over. However many hours you work as an employee there comes a point where you come home and leave it all behind you until the morning. (Or does there? BlackBerrys, laptops with mobile broadband dongles and other works of Satan all mean today's office worker is effectively on call 24 hours a day. I almost wept for the poor sod I saw coming home from London at 10.30 on a Friday evening, plugged into his laptop doing some spreadsheety thing and looking very, very sad about it.)

If you work at home, there is always that temptation to pop into the office, or fire up the laptop if you work at the kitchen table, and check your emails, fiddle with a bit of copy, post a comment to your blog, write a tweet or do any one of the myriad tasks we all find to fill up the time. Resist! Play with your kids if you have them. Go for a walk. Play tennis. Read a book. Have a glass of wine. Talk to your spouse, life-partner or significant other.

One of the things I love most about my job – and I love a lot of things about it – is that I pick my own hours. And by that I don't mean I goof off during the day but then work till three in the morning and at weekends. I almost never work in the evenings, and weekends are sacrosanct. I have a family and a social life and if I pop off this mortal coil tomorrow I don't want to be lounging around on a cloud with my wings on (well, I hope I'll have wings, not a pokey-pokey fork thing) saying "Yeah my last day on Earth was a Saturday spent writing a press release." I love my clients, but not that much.

Are you cut out to be a freelance copywriter?

A lot of people think they want to be freelance copywriters because they "love writing". That may well work for in-house copywriters, where someone else is handling all that tricky stuff such as finding clients and getting paid. But if you want to be a successful freelance copywriter, all the love in the world won't get you a penny in fees.

No. What you need is a love of running your own business. It's hard work, but when you land your first copywriting job, or your fiftieth, if I'm honest, there's a huge thrill. "I did this," you can shout. Me! So one of the strengths you're going to need is to be good at selling. Now we all talk about being salespeople for our clients, and we all quote John Kennedy's famous line about

When you land your first copywriting job, or your fiftieth, if I'm honest, there's a huge thrill.

advertising being "salesmanship in print". But we also have to be salespeople for ourselves, which a lot of people find very hard. A common problem is that we've never had to do it before. That degree in English was followed by a stint in an agency or client company, and now here we are, freelancing.

A couple of years after setting up Sunfish, I was having a beer with my friend and design guru Ross Speirs. As we sipped our pints of Shiftlock IPA, he leaned back and smiled, as only the long-term self-employed can, and uttered these words:

"Let's face it Andy, you're unemployable."

And he was right. He didn't mean I couldn't get hired. Just that I had passed beyond the world of corporate employment. You will too. You quickly become too concerned for your own quality of life – and work – to take another corporate job. Which means all this...

...no more bosses. No more meetings of such mind-numbing futility that you start giving yourself prison tats with a biro for light relief. No more memos or emails about the lifts not working. If this frightens you a little, take courage. This is a good thing. The world is full of people who are suited to corporate employment. It's just that it doesn't work for us.

If you're going to be a successful freelance copywriter you ... well, I suppose first we should decide what we mean by successful. Although much of this book, particularly the section on pricing your services, assumes that success is measured in financial terms, there are other ways of looking at it. Success might mean working three days a week. Or earning enough to pay for holidays, childcare and household bills. Or being respected. It's worth spending a little time deciding for yourself what you mean by successful. Because once you've done this, that's what you should aim for. After all, nobody wants to be unsuccessful.

I think being successful means establishing some measure of financial independence. It means being able to decide who to work for. It means working on your own terms. It means, ultimately, that you run a business you're proud of. So, back to my opening conditional clause.

If you're going to be a successful freelance copywriter you need a number of personal qualities. They are not the same qualities you need to be a successful copywriter. (Though you need these as well.)

Five things you need to be a successful copywriter

To be a successful copywriter you need:

- An abiding curiosity about people, the world around you and the products, services and companies you write for. Nothing is boring.
- The ability to understand how people think and feel about themselves and others. Without this you will struggle to sell – since this is the art of speaking to motivations.
- A talent for weaving magic with words, from story-telling to "what if?"; from a pell-mell rush of benefits to an irresistible call to action.
- Knowledge of the rules of spelling, grammar and punctuation – and the willingness and insight to know when you can – and should – break them.
- Research skills – from desk research to face-to-face interviewing – so you can uncover every single fact about whatever it is you're selling.

OK, let's have another go. If you're going to be a successful freelance copywriter you need seven personal qualities. Have a look at the list coming up and fill in the blank lines to give yourself a personal action plan.

Seven things you need to be a successful freelance copywriter

Put your business at the heart of your life. Invest in it. Financially as well as with your time.

1. Entrepreneurial spirit You've set up a business. So you need to act the way entrepreneurs do. Be willing to take risks, occasionally. Do deals. Put your business at the heart of your life. Invest in it. Financially as well as with your time. Yes, freelance copywriting can be a virtually overhead-free business, but you're missing a trick if you try to keep your spending down to the odd replacement toner cartridge and blog space upgrade. It might seem to you that spending £500 on a conference ticket is a bit steep. But who will you meet there – and how much could they spend with you in the lifetime of your business?

> My practical tip: from today, never again refer to (or think of) the money you make as pay or salary. It's either turnover, sales, revenue or profit. This will help you to think about what you're doing as running a business, not doing a job.

One action you'll take (write in something practical and measurable you can do to help with this quality):

_____

_____

_____

_____

_____

Deadline: _____

2. Thick skin However much you position yourself as an expert – whether in SEO (Search Engine Optimisation) copywriting, direct marketing or white papers; the financial services industry, high technology or pharmaceuticals – you will always come up against people who think they know more than you do. And because they are paying the bill, they believe that their views should prevail. This is the age-old problem: do you give your clients what they need – or what they want? When they reject your ideas, scribble all over your first draft or suggest that a page head reading "Welcome to our website" would be better than your superbly optimised version … you bite your tongue. You can try to persuade them of the rightness of your proposals; indeed, you must, if you're going to be a professional. But the old saying is true: he who pays the piper calls the tune. So don't sweat it. Make the changes, get the sign-off, raise the invoice and bank the cheque. It all spends the same.

> My practical tip: Create an A4 poster for your office/workspace that reads as follows: It's not personal, it's just business. Take a look at it when you're in the middle of a difficult conversation with a client.

One action you'll take (write in something practical and measurable you can do to help with this quality):

_____

_____

_____

_____

_____

Deadline: _____

3. Love of selling This is a hard one for some people to swallow. Even if you don't like the thought of selling, you must enjoy meeting new people, getting to know them and their problems, proposing solutions, negotiating fees and closing the sale (which is selling, after all). If you don't, you will forever be at the mercy of the skilled negotiators, business-savvy managers and assorted hardnuts who populate the clientosphere. It's not that you won't be busy if you can't sell, it's just that you will rarely be either working for what you're worth, or gaining much respect.

> My practical tip: remember that although you might feel you have a problem – lack of work/fee income – the person who really has the problem is your client. They have a website to launch or a marketing campaign to organise ... and nobody to write the copy. So you are the person who's going to make their worries disappear.

One action you'll take (write in something practical and measurable you can do to help with this quality):

_____

_____

_____

_____

_____

Deadline: _____

4. Business acumen Not quite the same as entrepreneurialism this. It's more to do with the ability to recognise sensible commercial decisions when they're staring you in the face. For example, not doing your own bookkeeping. Hiring someone to make sales calls for you if you don't like doing it yourself. Keeping a close eye on who owes you money and chasing unpaid invoices regularly and vigorously. And deciding what money you're going to spend on advertising in advance, rather than reacting to "special opportunities" presented to you by salesmen eager to meet their monthly targets.

> My practical tip: write a list of all the tasks that need doing in your business, apart from copywriting. Now

write someone's name against each of them ... and don't put your name more than twice.

One action you'll take (write in something practical and measurable you can do to help with this quality):

_____

_____

_____

_____

_____

Deadline: _____

5. Self-belief You can make a go of it as a freelance copywriter – if you have that elusive quality called confidence. How will you feel – and, more importantly, what will you do – when you have a quiet spell? Confidence means believing that every quiet spell is followed by a busy one. Confidence means not buckling under pressure when a new client suggests you cut your fee by 50 per cent. Confidence means going in to bat for your copy when a client starts querying or criticising it. Confidence doesn't mean being loud, aggressive or "salesy"; nor does it mean digging your heels in, being inflexible or boasting about how much success your other clients have had with your copy. You can be whoever you already are in terms of your personality – quiet, mild-mannered, whatever – just as long as you also have the belief in your abilities as a writer and a businessperson.

> My practical tip: write a list of all your achievements, personal, professional and commercial (probably not that 50-metre swimming badge). Pin it up where you can see it and make a point of reading it out loud once a week.

Confidence means believing that every quiet spell is followed by a busy one.

One action you'll take (write in something practical and measurable you can do to help with this quality):

_____

_____

_____

_____

_____

Deadline: _____

You need to be organised if you're going to run your own business.

6. Organisation You need to be organised if you're going to run your own business. Paperwork, especially financial paperwork, is going to start mushrooming, especially if you form a limited company. Clients will start raining work on you so you'll need some form of filing system, on your computer or in your office, to make sense of all those emails, project materials, drafts and proofs. What if you're not? No problem. Hire a virtual PA, pay your hyper-organised teenage daughter, buy lots of ring-binders.

My practical tip: Buy a filing cabinet. One drawer for client projects. One for financial paperwork. One for marketing. Use it.

One action you'll take (write in something practical and measurable you can do to help with this quality):

_____

_____

_____

_____

_____

Deadline: _____

7. Discipline How are you at deadlines? How about multiple deadlines? If you aspire to a life away from your keyboard, you're going to need a hefty dollop of self-discipline. The home office works against the focus you need to be successful. Doesn't mean it can't be done, just that you need to counter the gravitational pull of, well, almost everything else you can do at home and focus on getting great copy written on time. If you're not disciplined, you have a problem. Short of hiring someone to stand over you with a stick or handcuffing yourself to your desk, you're not going to cut it.

> My practical tip: Create a "to do" list on your computer – or your office wall. Book in every new job and every new enquiry. Devise a system of codes or tags so you know what stage each job/enquiry is at and what needs doing next.

One action you'll take (write in something practical and measurable you can do to help with this quality):

_____

_____

_____

_____

_____

Deadline: _____

Exercise 1
Freelance copywriter personality quiz

I thought it might be helpful to create one of those little personality tests you see in lifestyle magazines. It has no scientific rigour whatsoever, but will, I hope, give you some insight into whether you are cut out for the freelance copywriter's life. If you are already working as a freelance copywriter, you might find it fun anyway.

Simply circle the answer that applies most to you for each statement.*

1. I am happy to be by myself for large stretches of time with only a goldfish/pot plant/photo of my family for company.
    a) Agree strongly
    b) Agree
    c) Disagree
    d) Disagree strongly

2. If a client says they don't like what I've written, my reaction is to:
    a) Ask for specifics then go away and write a second draft incorporating their suggestions
    b) Tell them I didn't write it for them so what they like is irrelevant
    c) Start looking for a baseball bat
    d) Sit morosely in a corner considering a change in career
    e) Discuss their concerns with them, trying to persuade them to keep those elements I truly believe will make them sales, but giving way on other points of style or tone

3. I believe I am a good copywriter and worth every penny I charge for my services.

    a) Agree strongly

    b) Agree

    c) Disagree

    d) Disagree strongly

4. The most important skill I need as a freelance copywriter is:

    a) Being an excellent writer

    b) Knowing how to sell myself

    c) Psychological resilience

    d) Being an easy person to work with

    e) Being creative

5. When I think of marketing my business, my preferred channel is:

    a) Networking

    b) Social media

    c) Direct marketing

    d) Cold-calling

    e) Advertising

    f) Articles, blogs, books, speeches and training courses

6. The number of existing contacts I have that I can approach for copywriting work is:

    a) 0-5

    b) 6-15

    c) 16-30

    d) 30-50

    e) 50-99

    f) 100+

7. If I don't have any copywriting work coming in, I generally:
   a) Panic
   b) Pursue my hobbies
   c) Hit the phones
   d) Tweet about it
   e) Write an article about copywriting
   f) Set up some networking meetings

8. I see freelance copywriting as:
   a) A stepping stone to a job in an agency
   b) A way of filling in my CV until I get another corporate job
   c) A great way to earn money doing something I'm good at
   d) A chance to spend my time writing
   e) A way to get rich

9. I have a clear plan for marketing my copywriting business with well defined goals:
   a) Absolutely. Any bank would lend me money on the strength of it
   b) It's clear enough to give me confidence. I know where I'm going
   c) Kind of, but I don't always follow it.
   d) Not really, but I have a table napkin with "Ferrari in five years" written on it.
   e) Er, a what now?

10. If I won the lottery tomorrow, I would carry on working as a freelance copywriter:

   a) Are you crazy? It's off to the Caribbean, 1st class all the way.
   b) I don't know, do you think I could put my prices up?
   c) I would, but I'd be a damn sight choosier about which projects I took on.
   d) Absolutely, I love copywriting and can't imagine doing anything else.

See next page for scoring and analysis.

Scoring

1 a) 3, b) 2, c) 1, d) 0
2 a) 3, b) 2, c) 0, d) 1, e) 4
3 a) 3, b) 2, c) 0, d) -1
4 a) 2, b) 5, c) 3, d) 4, e) 1
5 a) 4, b) 1, c) 5, d) 6, e) 2, f) 3
6 a) 1, b) 2, c) 3, d) 4, e) 5, f) 6
7 a) 0, b) 2, c) 5, d) 1, e) 3, f) 4
8 a) 2, b) 1, c) 5, d) 3, e) 4
9 a) 4, b) 3, c) 1, d) 2, e) 0
10 a) 1 b) 2, c) 3, d) 4

Your score

31-45   Excellent! You have the right mixture of confidence, business savvy and stick-to-itiveness to work as a freelance copywriter.

21-30   Pretty good. This life can definitely work for you, but maybe look at those areas where you need to improve, especially on the business side of things.

11-20   Hmmm. You know, you could do well as a freelance. But you may have some work to do if you're really going to succeed.

0-10   Er, you know what, I heard there's a recruitment fair coming through town next month.

* Being a copywriter is all about curiosity, intuition and seeing the world from other people's perspectives. If you figured out the right answers and cheated to jack up your score, I reckon that's what qualifies you most of all. But then again, it's better to answer truthfully, because it's your life we're talking about here.

SECTION 2
SETTING UP IN BUSINESS AS A COPYWRITER

What you need is a love of running your own business.

First things first. If you're going to work for yourself you need to set up in business. Your first decision is whether to be a sole trader or form a limited company (or maybe a limited liability partnership, but for most of us it's a straight choice between the first two). You might think you're "just" a freelance copywriter, but the government, in the person of HM Revenue and Customs, will now start taking a little more interest in you. I don't want to go into exhaustive detail on the rigmarole of setting up a business, and all that tax stuff – there are lots of other books and websites that will tell you how – but let's take a quick look at some of the practical implications of this decision.

What kind of business are you going to be?

Sole trader

This means it's just you. No employees, not, technically, even yourself. No directors. No shareholders. It doesn't matter whether you give yourself a trading name – Inky Fingers Copywriting for example – or not. Your cheque book will say something like Chris Smith T/A Inky Fingers Copywriting. (T/A means "trading as".) Bookkeeping is simpler and cheaper for a sole trader. But any debts you incur are your personal responsibility. So if you end up owing a printer for a job that your client doesn't pay you for (perhaps because they go bust), you have to pay the printer regardless. If you can't afford it they can come after your personal assets. It's one of the reasons I opted to go Limited and also why, even now, I never buy print on behalf of clients. Yes, you can make a little commission on print buying, but for me, it's not worth the risk or the sleepless nights. In fact, the only time I did agree to buy print (for a large government department) I asked them to pay me up front based on the printer's quotation. There is a perception among some clients – and among quite a few sole traders themselves – that sole traders look "small". It's harder to tender for and win large contracts as a sole trader.

Limited company

The clue is in the name. Your company has limited liabilities. Providing the directors don't knowingly trade when the business is insolvent (ie. unable to pay its debts) your liabilities extend only to the assets of the company. They can take your printer and your laptop, but your flat, car and vintage dress collection are all fine. Now you have to file "proper" annual reports and accounts every year. You have to behave according to the law as it affects company directors. You will need to hire an accountant (I'd advise doing that anyway – more on this later). And you will have to spend more on admin costs. On the credit side, you will also look "big". Or "bigger". There's a branding opportunity here to position yourself as a substantial business, regardless of whether it's still just you and your MacBook in the attic. And you get to put Managing Director, Creative Director or Chief Wordsmithery Director, if the mood takes you, on your business cards.

Where are you going to work?

Ah, yes. Your office. For many freelancers, not just in copywriting, but design, project management, gardening, photography and the rest, your office can be one of the following:

- The kitchen table
- A corner of the sitting room where you've squeezed in an IKEA desk and a filing cabinet
- Starbucks
- Anywhere with free public Wi-Fi
- The box room
- The attic

- A dedicated room in your flat or house
- A desk or office sublet from a local firm eg. accountants, designers
- An office in a business centre

I'd advise you to go for the quietest space you can find. Not necessarily the biggest, though a little more space is always welcome. My first office was the small bedroom in our flat in West London. If I leaned back in my chair and did a sort of snow-angel pose I could touch all four walls simultaneously (that's feet, hands and head if you're trying to picture it). But it was at least my space. Not MySpace, that wasn't invented then.

In the early days money is going to be tight or, at least, feel tight. Lashing out £350 a week for 50 square feet of serviced offices will give you the trappings of success, but before you've earned the money to enjoy them. After 14 years I still work from home, albeit in a purpose-built office, because a) I can't bear paying for something I already have, and b) when I'm not writing, I'm already back with the family and my guitars.

Most important of all, you need to create a space that feels businesslike.

Most important of all, you need to create a space that feels businesslike. If you're serious about making money as a freelance, you need to treat the whole thing with as much professionalism as you can muster. If there are children in your life, you have a big challenge. When I started out we were free of ankle-biters and had the luxury of arranging our lives around work and socialising. Now the whole thing takes a little more work. Office door closed means daddy is at work. Office door open means quiet visits permitted.

What equipment do you need?

As with the tax thing, I don't propose to fill up pages listing every item of stationery you need to buy. I, personally, am a stationery junkie and will happily fill a trolley in Staples when all I went in for was a couple of toner cartridges. You can make your own choices here I feel. But again there are a few decisions that have business consequences.

Your phone

Get a dedicated line for your business. Either that or face clients having to compete with your friends and family for your time, and risk your five-year-old answering the phone to a potential £10K client. A mobile is good, but remember, even now, people tend to place more trust in a firm with a landline. It doesn't look so fly-by-night. And record a sensible, professional, out-of-office voicemail message. Not, as I have heard, the standard phone company message "Hello, the person you are calling is out. Please leave your message after the tone." Forgive me if this sounds Noddy to you, but when you pick up, remember your client thinks they are calling a business. Here's a form of words that sends the right message:

> Good morning/afternoon: Inky Fingers Copywriting. Give it an upwards inflexion at the end to signal them to start talking.
> Or this...
> Chris Smith. (said assertively like important business types do when you get through to their direct line)
> But not this...
> Hello?

Or this...

> Er, [cough cough], gosh sorry had my mouth full of sandwich. (I have heard this. Yes, truly I have).

41

Your desk

It doesn't have to be expensive. Mine is the original makeshift bench I built when I started out: a huge piece of black-painted medium density fibreboard resting on two second-hand credenzas (Is that what they're called? Drawer things, anyway). It does have to fit the way you work. If you're the minimalist, scorched-earth type, a small desk is fine, with somewhere to keep papers and work in progress. If you're the messy, "I know it's here somewhere", type (and I'm trying not to be judgmental here though I think I may be suffering from a little verbal leakage) you might want to consider something bigger, with more storage. If you can, have a desk that is yours. Sharing it with your spouse, kids or plates of pasta is a recipe for lost drafts, misplaced client messages and more stress (which you really don't need).

Your chair

Unlike your desk, which is essentially just a plank for resting your PC on, your chair is critical. You're going to be spending a lot of hours on it so make sure it's comfortable. More importantly, make sure it's a proper, orthopaedically designed chair. I spent a small fortune on mine, but it's probably paid for itself in saved visits to the chiropractor.

Your computer

In the UK, most copywriters seem to use PCs, which, I think, is a shame, given their performance relative to Macs. But at any rate, buy a decent one, the fastest and most specced-up you can afford. I use a desktop most of the time. I suspect this is partly a function of age – I am not the laptop generation. I also like the big keyboard and the ability to have my screen at eye level so I don't have to look down all the time. What you choose is up to you but again, make sure it's yours. One day I went to a meeting and turned on my laptop (I do own one, I just don't use it much) only to find "someone" had installed on it a burger chain's freebie desktop wallpaper .

Much more important than your PC though is your backup drive. Because you're going to want to get one. In the early days I lost a lot of live projects when my PC's hard-drive fried in the middle of the night. I was told that for a modest fee, some Russian "security consultants" could probably recover it, but I just rewrote everything instead. I now use a Maxtor One-touch which is about the size of a pack of cards and worth every penny I paid for it. I have recovered documents that disappeared when my PC had a hissy fit several times and I can also back up all my emails and contacts. Priceless.

Your stationery

When I started out I had letterheads, compliment slips and business cards printed – the classic stationery set you can get as a special deal from most firms of local printers. You really don't need a letterhead printing these days – though getting a design you can use in Word is a good idea for invoices, quotations etc. Comp slips? Well, they're useful if you're sending samples to a prospect in the post. I switched to A7 sticky notes printed with our logo a while ago – they're much cheaper, more flexible in the ways you can use them and double up as giveaways. But business cards? Aha! Now we get into interesting territory.

The best piece of advice I ever read about business cards was in a newsletter from our bank. It said, "use all the space – print on the back". Now this will cost you more. A little bit more. But it is an investment. Picture the scene. You're at a networking meeting and you hand your card to a prospective client. This is what happens next.

They turn it over.

So what will they see on your card? Nothing? Or a miniature poster advertising and selling your copywriting services?

The best piece of advice I ever read about business cards was in a newsletter from our bank. It said, "use all the space – print on the back".

I now have a fairly busy diary delivering copywriting and business writing training courses. All because when I started out I had the words "training courses" printed on the back of my business card. A client rang me after a meeting and booked four.

What are you going to call yourself?

Another big decision, this one: what to call yourself. Professionally I mean. There are three broad schools of thought on good business names for copywriters – judging by my trawls through the web.

1. Use your own name

This creates an instant brand. It's likely to be unique and registrable as a domain name. You can also use it as a company name if you go down the Ltd route. It can make you sound like what you are a one-person micro-business, but then again, it worked for Leo Burnett and J. Walter Thompson. Of course, you may have a name that you feel doesn't quite fit the bill, however much you like it. If you're Artemis J. Craphowler III you're probably going to be brainstorming some other names for the business.

You can also tag "copywriting" onto the end if you want to create something a little more business-y. Dee Jones Copywriting sounds pretty good to my ears.

2. Play around with "copy", "write" and other write-y words

Lots of copywriters go down this route. It's kinda cute because we can show we're creative with language just in the name we've chosen for our copywriting business. But if you're starting out now, you have to be supercreative because a lot of the good ones have already gone. Take a look at my interviewees' company names for proof.

As a counter-argument, you don't have to explain what you do with your company name. Nike, Remington, Barbour, Rolls Royce, Orange: they all manage. Because remember, you will be building a pretty sophisticated sales and marketing strategy, so your name only really has to be something that sticks in the client's mind.

3. Come up with something abstract, conceptual or unrelated to the business of writing

My business is called Sunfish. I knew I didn't want to be called Andy Maslen & Associates because I thought it wasn't enough of a brand (shows how much I knew about branding!). I also didn't know that I would end up specialising in copy. Back then I also did a lot of consulting, marketing audits, sales training, you name it. Sunfish didn't pigeonhole me.

A lot of agencies work this way. Geronimo, St Luke's, Mother, Joshua ... the list goes on. This approach gives you an instant talking point as everyone will ask you the same question, "So, Mustang, where did that come from?" Then all you need is a convincing explanation for the name and some clever relation to copywriting. "Wild horses wouldn't drag us away from copywriting." I still don't have one for Sunfish.

Take your time on this one: you'll be stuck with it for the rest of your life. Can you say it without stumbling over it? When you say it, do people hear it accurately? Do you have to spell it out? Does it have any weird, funny or negative connotations? Is the .com, .co.uk or .net available? (If not it's a non-starter to be honest.) Would you be happy standing up in front of a seminar audience and introducing yourself as boss of <name>?

Are you going to specialise?

Let's be honest. If you're just starting out as a freelance copywriter, specialising is not going to be a priority. You will be more concerned (I'm guessing here) with landing paying work. Any paying work. So you'll be a generalist. Or will you? Maybe your background in a particular industry means you can sell your expertise in writing for oil companies, pharmaceutical firms, IT companies, accountants or publishers. Perhaps in your last job you were the web marketing manager so you can specialise in online copywriting. Or the head of PR, so you know loads about writing press releases, articles and white papers. Even if you have no industry or business experience at all, you can always decide to specialise in whatever form of copywriting you find most attractive.

Just because you specialise, doesn't mean you can't pitch for, or quote for, jobs that fall outside your special field of interest.

Just because you specialise, doesn't mean you can't pitch for, or quote for, jobs that fall outside your special field of interest. But for all those clients looking for that kind of expertise, you're going to look more attractive. I have never worked for an agency and never freelanced for them, but I can imagine that if you specialise in working for agencies, and get to know their particular ways of working and disciplines, you will pick up more work from them.

My advice is to decide on something to specialise in. When those jobs come up in the market, you will be more likely get onto the pitch list (if there is one) and more likely to get hired. When these jobs don't, but others do, you can explain that your core skills of research, customer insight and wordsmithing are ultratransferable. Most clients want a copywriter who is more knowledgeable and skilled than they are – and who will do a good job. Aiming to be a specialist (and having some form of evidence to back it up) is a good way to start.

No more water-cooler: building your network

I think many new freelancers, and probably many established ones, struggle to replace the informal social networks and casual human contact you get at work. Work in a corporate office I mean. If you are by nature more of a loner (not the kind with a sniper rifle and six months' worth of tinned goods in your cabin in the woods, just someone who's happy with his/her own company) you have a distinct advantage over your more gregarious peers.

As a freelance you can find yourself looking forward to those letters that need signing for, just so you can engage the postman in conversation. FedEx deliveries become springboards for new and rewarding friendships (or so you fondly think). And chance encounters in the street as you go to post your latest invoice take on a significance that would startle your former colleagues.

It's important to have a close network of friends and colleagues whom you can meet now and again for a coffee and a chat. And I mean in real life. Twitter, Facebook, LinkedIn and the rest all give the illusion of company, but they're a pale reflection of the real thing. So join local networking groups. Keep in touch with your friends who also work for themselves. More and more of us are doing it now, but even in the mid-Nineties when I started out, at least as many of my friends were freelancing as employed in corporate jobs.

And yes, tweet away like your life depended on it. Just remember that a half-hour break for coffee with a friend is far less disruptive and a lot more fulfilling than 15 random two-minute breaks to post something online.

Time management

So you've started your own freelance copywriting business. Now your time's your own. Or is it? Your clients may see it differently, expecting you to work round the clock or over the weekend to get their work done. Your spouse, if you have one, may see your new home-based status as a Godsend. "Oh, darling," they smile, as they swing out the front door to their cushy job in town, "could you take my suit to the dry cleaners for me? Oh, and we've run out of linguine too." Your children (see spouse above) will rock through the front door at 3.30 or 4.00 – maybe you've had to knock off for half an hour to collect them – and start demanding milk and cookies or, if they're paragons, help with their homework. No, no, no! None of this will do. And none of it will work.

One way or another you have to set boundaries. Whatever your life looks like, however many other souls live with you, from pets to offspring, you have to make it clear to them – and yourself – that you are working. Even if you set two two-hour periods in the day as your business hours, stick to them and make sure everybody else does too. Once the fees start rolling in, it's a lot easier to persuade everyone that you need space and time to work, by the way.

And recognise that you have competing demands on your time even when you are left to get on with it. In the olden days when I started out you had three options for filling your time. You could write copy. You could try to win some work. You could go for a walk. A copywriter I was speaking to recently bemoaned the fact she had to parcel out her time between writing copy, blogging, reading stuff she'd found on the web, updating her various online profiles … you get the picture.

In terms of priorities, I think they should run something like this:

1st   Deliver copy you're being paid to write, on time and to a high standard.

2nd   Follow up on any leads you have, especially people you've spoken to once already.

3rd   Invoice any jobs you've finished.

4th   Chase late payments.

5th   Pitch for new work.

6th   Deal with any reputation-boosting opportunities eg. speeches, articles for magazines, seminars, training courses.

7th   Write or update your publicity materials: blog, website, e-zine, tweets.

I find I have two times of day when I am best able to write copy. From 8.00 am to 11.30 am and from 4.00 pm to about 6.00. So that's when I write. There's an almost audible click in my head just after that morning coffee break when I lose my copywriting mojo. Which is fine. I have usually cracked whatever it is I'm working on and am happy to switch to business tasks. Identify your writing times and use them for writing. Block that time out, switch your phone off and please, if you haven't already, reconfigure your email program so you choose when to check emails. Nothing is going to disrupt your productivity more thoroughly, more effectively, more constantly, than repeated "bings" or "bongs" to let you know that "you have mail". Believe me, it can wait.

This issue of productivity may be new to you, it may not. But as we'll see in the section on pricing your services, it's crucial in determining the money you can make and everything that flows from that. Whether you bill by the hour or by the project, these are the only hours you have to make money in and if you fritter them away, that's it. No fee income.

Identify your writing times and use them for writing. Block that time out, switch your phone off and choose not to check for emails during this time.

Copyright, contracts and terms of business

As a former barrack-room lawyer, policing infringements of copyright for the publisher I worked for, I got to know more about contracts and copyright law than I probably now need. But I did learn a couple of very important things for freelance copywriters. Here they are.

Copyright

When you create an original "work", such as a piece of writing, a photograph or a painting, you own the copyright. Automatically. You can't "copyright" something. Partly because copyright isn't a verb, it's a noun, and partly because it's not up to you. It just happens. That's the law. You can register something as a trademark, which is where I suspect some people get confused, but even here, let's be precise with our language and agree that the verb is register not trademark.

So, you write a web page or a brochure for a client. Guess who owns the copyright? That's right. You do. (Unless you have explicitly assigned it to the client). Which I think you'll agree is an interesting state of affairs. They pay you all that money yet they don't own the work. What they do have is what's called an "implied right" to use the copy. That means, it's clear from the contract, which may only be oral, that they were paying you to write copy for their website because they would be using it in that way. It's usually not a problem and in my experience very rarely gets discussed, but it's there and it's something worth knowing about. In my terms of business, I specifically state that Sunfish Ltd retains the copyright until the client pays their bill. At which point copyright is assigned to the client. Between those points, the client has the exclusive licence to use the copy, in other words, I won't let anyone else have it.

Now this may all seem like rather abstruse legal jargon for us lowly copywriters, but court cases have been fought over copyright in advertising campaigns. You can also use it as a lever when you are facing a client who is tardy with the payment for your work; pointing out sweetly that they don't own the copyright can be just the tickle up they need.

Contracts

We've mentioned contracts and terms of business, so let's take a quick look at these two items in your business set-up. Every job you do for a client is governed by a contract. If you don't have a written one, you have an oral one. And it's pedantry time again. A verbal contract can be written or spoken. Verbal means to do with words, as opposed to a numerical or pictorial or body language contract. Oral means spoken – literally from the mouth – and it's surprising how many copywriting contracts exist in this form only. My advice to you: get it in writing. You can have a simple exchange of emails, an attachment in Word that the client signs and returns, a 40-page legal document, whatever.

Why should freelance copywriting be the only industry that doesn't use contracts to regulate relationships between buyers and sellers? They're great for setting out exactly what each party has agreed to do. At its simplest, the contract will state that you are going to use your best efforts to write a standout piece of copy and your client is going to pay you X for it. How much you put into it is up to you, but here are a few things to consider, including:

- The format and extent of the copy
- The goal of the copy
- The deadline
- How you are going to get the information you need
- How many drafts you are going to do
- Whether and how often you will meet the client face-to-face
- The fee
- Payment terms
- Copyright

It seems obvious to me that your contract should be proportionate to the size of the job and likely complexity. If you agree to write a menu for a local restaurant, which I did once, a one-line email, or even a phone conversation if you get on well, is fine. If you agree to write an entire launch campaign for a new multimillion pound product, you may feel a little more paper is required.

Incidentally, unless you are extremely confident in your abilities, and have complete control over the entire marketing campaign in which your copy appears, and the product you are promoting, I would leave out of any contract the idea that you guarantee results. You hope for results, of course, but it's a mistake to commit yourself legally to delivering them.

Terms of business

You put in your terms of business everything you think is important about taking on a job and a client.

Terms of business is really just a fancy phrase meaning "the way we do things around here" or "how we work". But it's worth writing some and including them as part of every contract. You put in your terms of business everything you think is important about taking on a job and a client. Some of those items are in the list above. But you can also add stuff in about conflicts of interest, late payment fees, exactly how long you are prepared to wait for amendments before charging separately for them and so on. Then there is less room for debate about who agreed to do what for whom. If your client has emailed you saying, in essence, "Yes, you're hired on that basis", it's easier to keep everyone on the same page (literally) should there be a dispute later on.

Lest you feel all this stuff about contracts and disputes is a bit doom-and-gloom, I should point out that from 1996 until the time of writing, we have been involved in precisely no court cases and no disputes. Clients have, on perhaps a handful of occasions, asked for a reduction in the fee, based on some perceived mismatch between copy and brief. In those cases we have usually given way. Why? Partly because life's too short.

Partly because the sums involved were not huge. And partly for reasons of goodwill and the feeling that in the long term we have more to gain by being amenable (within limits) rather than litigious. I know not every copywriter shares that view (or indeed experience). It may also be that we have suffered less from legal stuff precisely because we have always tried to use contracts.

Conflicts of interest, what are they and do they matter?

I think it's as well to consider the idea of conflicts of interest before you get too far down the road. What do I mean by conflict of interest? Although there are all sorts of financial and moral definitions, all I mean is when you might be working for two direct competitors at the same time. I have never done that – I honestly couldn't find a way to square that with my sense of fair play. After all, if you have a blinding idea who's going to get it? I guess you might also have a conflict of interest if you owned shares in a printing company you advised a client to use, without disclosing your interest. But come on, has that ever happened to a freelance copywriter? I doubt it.

Back to our first example. Would you feel comfortable taking on work from two direct competitors, one after the other? If you're not on a retainer then it's entirely up to you. One of the joys of freelancing is you get to choose your own clients. If they don't want you to work for a competitor, then it's really up to them to include that term in your contract. In all the years I have been running Sunfish, it's never come up. But I do have a paragraph in our terms of business that explicitly states that we won't take on a project that would create a conflict of interest. Just a little bit of reassurance for the client.

SECTION 3
DEALING WITH MONEY

It doesn't matter which kind of money manager you are, just so long as you recognise your type.

There's a really important shift in attitudes you have to make when you start your own business. From now on, forget about salary. You should be thinking about either turnover (sales) or profit (sales less costs). This will help you think like a businessperson and not just a jobbing freelance. You may feel that getting £300 for a day's work is too good to be true, but when your printer and laptop both need replacing in the same month, your pension contribution falls due, and you've paid your own travel expenses for five client meetings, that £300 starts to look like peanuts. Do not compare your rates to either your last salary or that of your clients. They don't have a business to run: you do. OK, sermon over. Let me ask you a question…

What role does money play in your life?

You can get rich being a freelance copywriter. You can also get poor. And you can be somewhere in the middle.

You can get rich being a freelance copywriter. You can also get poor. And you can be somewhere in the middle. So before we get onto the subject of winning work and pricing it, we need a little digression on the subject of filthy lucre itself. What is your attitude to money? Are you motivated by its mere possession – big bank balances and the like? Is it what you can buy with it – nice car outside the house, swanky holidays? Is it the security it affords – family looked after, insurances up to date, decent pension salted away? Is it a proxy for professional standing and recognition – "I must be a good copywriter, I made £50,000 last year"? I think it helps to spend a little time thinking about your attitude to money and how much of the stuff you need – and want.

Suppose your aim is, initially, to replace your salary (despite what I said in the opening to this section). A long time ago now I read an article about being a consultant, when that's what I thought I'd be doing. It pointed out that you couldn't simply take your old salary and divide it by 52, then by 5, and say "There. That's my daily rate".

Here's why.

- Assume Jay has just given up his job as a marketing manager. His salary was £30,000 a year.
- Using the simple formula above Jay calculates his daily rate as £115.
- But hang on. Jay used to get four weeks' paid holiday a year. So really he should be dividing by 48, not 52. That ups the daily rate to £125.
- But what about pension contributions? And sick pay? The subsidised gym membership? And National Insurance (NI)? Let's not even get into the occasional free biro.
- OK, thinks Jay, I better jack it up to £150 – that should cover those extras.
- So armed with his new daily rate and a box of business cards, Jay sets about his consulting business. And finds he's working about one day in three. (Which is pretty good, by the way.)
- One evening, he sits down with his calculator and runs the numbers.
- 48 weeks multiplied by 5 equals 240 potential fee-earning days.
- I work one in three days which means an annual total of 80 days.
- At £150 a day that means I'm going to make £12,000 this year. Aaaghh!

So Jay goes back to the drawing board and triples his daily rate. That's right, he triples it. To £450. Now the sums yield his old salary plus a bit more.

As far as I can remember it, the article set out a formula for calculating your daily rate. It went something like this:

DR = (FS/230) x 1.20 x 3

Where DR is daily rate and FS is final salary.

The 230 is the maximum number of billable days in the year (allowing for your holidays, public holidays and weekends), the

1.2 covers all those things your employer used to pay for, and the 3 covers the fact you are budgeting to be doing fee-paying work one day in three.

For Jay, that would give a daily rate of $(30,000/230) \times 1.2 \times 3 = £469.57$. Let's call it £500 a day.

Now, what is the significance of all this for freelance copywriters? A lot of freelancers I talk to price their services (even if they don't charge for them) by the hour. Whether you explicitly account for your time or just use it as an internal accounting system, it means, on average, you need to be billing at a nominal daily rate of £500 if you want an equivalent income of £30,000 a year.

If you can write productively for ten hours a day, every day, your hourly rate can be £50. If, like me, you struggle to write anything of any quality for more than four hours a day (because you are also striving to bring in new business, follow up on quotes and generally run your business), your hourly rate needs to be £125. I'm not sure how many clients or agencies would be willing to hire a freelance copywriter who quoted that as their rate. I'll leave this thought with you for now because we are going to cover pricing your services in more detail in Section 4. Just bear in mind that £30,000 is a fairly modest ambition for someone with the skills you possess.

Who's going to look after the books?

Some people are very good at managing their money. They balance their cheque books at the end of every month and they always know exactly how much money they have in the bank. Others are a little more free and easy. Maybe a bit overdrawn here and there, maybe robbing Peter to pay Paul occasionally, but usually OK. And for some people, money seems to slip through their fingers like sand.

Once again, it doesn't really matter which kind of money manager you are, just so long as you recognise your type. If you're superorganised with money, you have the option of doing your own bookkeeping, invoicing, VAT returns and all the rest. If you're more chaotic, you should hire or find someone who will look after it all for you. That could be a spouse, but there are also plenty of qualified people out there who offer bookkeeping services for a modest fee. And you reap two benefits. First, you have the confidence and reassurance that your financial affairs are in good order. Second, you get to spend your time on what you do best – copywriting – not being a second or third-rate accountant. You do have to share some fairly intimate details of your financial affairs (like how much you earn), but that's the choice you take. And at some point I hope you're going to be successful enough that you'll need to hire an accountant, at which point they will have a legal right and responsibility to know what you earn, so the problem disappears.

I'd count myself as a pretty good money manager, and although our accountants did the annual report and accounts for Sunfish for ten years, I always handled the sales and purchase ledgers, the cash book, PAYE stuff and the VAT return. Then I realised one day that I could earn more in fees during the time I spent bookkeeping than I'd be paying our accountants to do it for us. Now I send every last bit of official paper to them once a month and go back to my work. Perfect.

Billing isn't banking

The real question, and the one you should be asking yourself, is, "How much have I banked this month?" .

There's something incredibly exciting about raising your first invoice. Wow, I'm making money, you think. Or, possibly, shout. But you're not. All you've done so far is type another document. OK it has some legal force but an invoice in your client's hands is a very different matter from a bunch of twenties in yours. So let's not get all romantic about invoices. "I've billed £2,000 this month," is not as great as it sounds. The real question, and the one you should be asking yourself, is, "How much have I banked this month?" Yes, debts (money owed to you, I mean) appear on your balance sheet and they are an asset of the business in dry financial terms, but you can't spend them in Tesco.

All this means you have to get good at credit control. Or chasing debts in other words. And you have two options here. Option one is to go back to your client, a marketing manager, for example, and politely point out that you haven't been paid. Here's a suggested form of words for an email:

> *Hi Jodie,*
>
> *I thought you might want to know that our invoice #555 for your HTML email hasn't been paid yet. It was due for payment on 31 October.*
> *I know it isn't your job, but I wonder whether you'd mind giving your accounts department a prod for us.*
>
> *Thanks and best regards,*
> *Andy*

They will be embarrassed, having probably assumed that since they signed off your invoice a few weeks ago, it would have been paid by now. They are also the person with whom you have the relationship, and if all is going well, will want to help you out and be indignant on your behalf.

Even if you suspect that they themselves are holding things up, this is an effective first step, since it gives them a chance to clear the debt.

Option two is to chase the accounts payable department or person directly. Now you are plugged directly into the person who types your details into the accounting software for the BACS (Bankers Automated Clearing System) or cheque run. Get them on your side and they will probably be eager to help you. For them, this is just a transaction: no emotional content, just data. Remember that.

For both of these scenarios, I am thinking of larger organisations. If you work for start-ups or small businesses, your client may be the MD and the person who organises payments. They may be short of cash that month or just slow to pay on purpose. Here, I think, diplomacy is your first approach, but remember your contract. They agreed to pay you and you are legally entitled to be paid. By the time you are chasing this kind of person for payment, your options are somewhat limited. It's far better to screen potential clients before you start working for them to get a sense of their likelihood to pay. If you have terms of business that state you expect to be paid after 30 days (which is common, but, when you think about it, outrageous that you should be offering interest-free credit to a multinational company for a month), you have to decide what you're going to do once the debt starts "ageing". Sending a statement every month is an idea if you are sending in multiple invoices each month to the same company. But if it's just one invoice, phone calls and emails as soon as the 30 days are up will probably be more effective. For us at Sunfish, 90 days is the cut-off point. As it approaches, we will send a friendly but firm email that says something like this:

Dear Jodie,

I thought you would want to know that our invoice #555 remains unpaid and is now at 85 days.

It's our policy, once an invoice reaches 90 days, to begin legal proceedings to recover the debt.

Please could you have a word with your accounts department and let me know when we can expect to be paid.

Best regards,
Andy

The tone is still polite, though marginally less friendly, and the language is more assertive than our earlier email. Phrases such as "legal proceedings" and "recover the debt" are there deliberately, not to frighten the client, whom we like, but to be on the record, since this email will almost certainly be forwarded to the accounts department and possibly the finance director. I have found it works. And we have only ever used it three times since starting the agency. I tend to feel if it gets this far we have dropped the ball in terms of keeping in touch with the client.

Tax

Imagine reading that section head while screeching Hitchcockian violins go "eee eee eee" in the background. I couldn't leave this section without a brief word on tax. For many freelancers – in any trade – it's the taxman who causes most of their problems. Which is kind of unfair, because he was always there, doing what taxmen do. It's just that you didn't notice because all your income tax was deducted at source before you saw your hard-earned cash. Now, though, you are responsible for paying your own tax. And the big takeaway message here is: always put some money aside for tax. If you're a sole trader it's all income tax; if you are a limited company, you also have to allow for corporation tax. I knew a guy many years ago who would have a fantastic year … then spend all the money. He assumed that this good year would be followed by another one, and he would pay this year's tax bill out of next year's money. But sometimes he would have a crap year next year. Cue panicked raiding of piggy banks and fishing down the back of the sofa.

The taxman doesn't care what sort of year you're having this year. He just wants his money from <u>last</u> year. In fact it's a bit more complicated than that, as you find yourself paying last year's bill, plus a bit on account for this year. The taxman assumes that if last year was good, this year will be too. Before we disappear up our own tax returns trying to figure all this out, here's the only thing you really need to remember about the money you make as a freelance copywriter:

It. Isn't. All. Yours.

Talk to your accountant about the proportion you should set aside for tax. And then set it aside. Put it in a deposit account and swear to yourself on your copy of Scientific Advertising that you won't touch it. Until it's time to pay your tax. Then you'll feel happy.

For many freelancers, it's the taxman who causes most of their problems... The big takeaway message here is: always put some money aside for tax.

SECTION 4
WINNING YOUR FIRST COPYWRITING JOB

Remember that if you're good at selling, you may get paying work without the need to show samples.

Right. Now for the good stuff. If you're new to the freelance game, this is probably what you bought this book for, so my apologies for keeping you waiting. First, a warning. Although it's an unfashionable concept these days, what with social media an' all, to get your first copywriting job, **you're going to have to hustle**.

If you have built a thriving copywriting practice on the back of Twitter or Facebook, email me and I will a) ring you and pick your brains to find out how you did it, and b) interview you for the next edition of this book.

By hustle I mean cold call. I mean keep your business cards in your pocket and make sure you give them out to people who could hire you, wherever you meet them. Be persistent and pull every lever you've got to win the job. If a prospective client asks you for a sample of a website you've written, and you've yet to win a paid web writing gig, show them a site you wrote for practice. And be ready for Martini selling: any time, any place, anywhere (oops, showing my age there). Soon after we had relocated to Salisbury from London, we were meeting some new friends for dinner in an Indian restaurant in town. I knew Giles was the finance director of a big company based in Salisbury. So as we were standing at the bar I asked him who I should talk to in the marketing department at his company. "You can talk to me," he said. So I did. And even after seven years working for myself I found I was somewhat unprepared to launch into my pitch. Don't let this happen to you. Have your elevator pitch ready, and a longer version too.

I'm sure you know what an elevator pitch is. If you don't have that ten-second verbal logo at the ready, now would be a good time to write one. Right now, I mean. What you want is a line that succinctly captures what you do, for whom, and why that's important. If you can also include some sort of unique fact or quality that will distinguish you from AN Other copywriter, so much the better.

> **Keep your business cards in your pocket and make sure you give them out to people who could hire you, wherever you meet them.**

Here's your opening bit of dialogue:

Exercise 2 – The elevator pitch

A first-class train compartment. The train glides into a station. A smartly dressed businesswoman sits down next to you, a freelance copywriter.

> SDB: Lovely weather we're having.
> FC: Yes. I thought we might have more rain.
> *[It's two British people talking: you can tell.]*
> SDB looks over at blank but branded document on FC's laptop.
> SDB: Inkwell. That's an interesting name. What do you do?
> FC: I_____
> _____.

So, what are you going to say to her? Here are a few thoughts.

You could say what you are. Like this:

I am a freelance copywriter.

Huh?

You could say what you do. Like this:

I write the copy that goes on companies' websites and marketing materials.

She's in HR so this leaves her cold and she turns back to her copy of the *Financial Times*.

You could focus on the results you get for your clients. Like this:

I help companies sell more.

This is better, though vague as to how you do it, and it still leaves her cold.

And although you might feel she's "only" in HR, she is a director of the company and meets regularly with the marketing director, so you are really missing a trick here. Try to come up with something that would give you an in with this businesswoman, or any other executive, regardless of their personal responsibilities, and which would make them ask for your card.

Back to building your business from scratch, and I guess I was lucky in this regard. I had been working in marketing within the business information publishing industry for a dozen years or so, which meant I had lots of contacts. I had also been working at a fairly senior level, so I found it easier to get in front of the people who would give me work. If that applies to you, it's a real bonus. But either way, there are a few things you need to decide on before you get going.

How are you going to decide whom to write for?

We've already talked a bit about specialising. It helps, I think, but in the early days you tend to take what you can find. Or else you starve. Let's face it, if a client offers you a website to write, you're hardly likely to turn it down because you specialise in corporate brochures. Here are a few things you might want to think about.

Are there any industries or products you would feel uncomfortable writing for? There are businesses catering for every human need. Not all of them particularly savoury. And they all have websites, AdWord campaigns, e-books and the rest. They might want you to write the copy for them. How do you feel about that? I have certain products I won't work on, but that's a personal choice and should be of zero concern to you. I know copywriters who won't take on work from tobacco companies, get-rich-quick schemes, oil companies or whatever offends their sense of ethics. You just need to decide where you draw the line. It helps when fielding calls from prospective clients and you might even put a line or two on your website. It just saves time.

Are you happy to work for start-ups/one-man/woman bands? No offence intended by the following comparison, but, just like porn websites, gambling sites, herbal Viagra suppliers and repressive regimes, start-ups need copy too. Here the problem isn't one of ethics or even aesthetics, but cold, hard cash. The upside is you are dealing with a client who passionately believes in the value of their product. You could be in on the start of something big. And you can almost feel like you're part of the team. The downside is that team may not be paying themselves, and they may expect you to act in the same generous spirit, offering you shares, or a royalty on sales or commission instead of a fee. This may not be your experience, but I have found this type of client expects a disproportionate amount of hand-holding, is more likely to quibble over fees, and will extract free marketing consultancy from you. As a result I tend to screen them more carefully than I do marketing managers from medium to large organisations. I accept that this may be an unfair approach.

Are you going to focus on your local market? With the possible exception of those based in London (or other major world cities such as New York), many freelance copywriters seem to work for clients based mainly in their own town, city or region. Kind of makes sense. I mean if you're based in Newtown, you're going to want to join the Newtown chamber of commerce, call the creative directors of all the Newtown graphic design and advertising agencies and possibly mail the marketing managers of all the businesses based in Newtown. But if that's the approach you take, you are limiting yourself severely. Copywriting is the ultimate borderless job. You can email the product anywhere in the world and you can do business exclusively by phone and email. Focusing on an industry, on the other hand, allows you to build up a reputation among a community of clients wherever they're based.

> **Copywriting is the ultimate borderless job. You can email the product anywhere in the world and you can do business exclusively by phone and email.**

Aesthetic, ethical and marketing questions to one side, your main criterion for selecting clients (and remember it's as much this way round as them selecting you) is this:

Will they pay you?

Your secondary criterion is:

Will they pay you on time?

There's an old business saying that we should all have tattooed on our foreheads, "sales are vanity, profits are sanity". But we can adapt it slightly and say "clients are vanity, settled accounts are sanity". Now, why did that never catch on?

Whether your clients are big or small, multinational or start-up, down the road or half-way up the Amazon, you need to feel sure that you will get paid. Bankruptcies to one side, there are fewer risks attendant on working for larger organisations than smaller ones. Mainly because payment is part of a process. To the person who has just taken out a second mortgage on their home and not paid themselves for a year, payment is personal. That said, the clients we have threatened with court have all been very, very big.

All it means is you have to apply some common (business) sense when taking on a new client. Try to get a sense of their willingness and ability to pay before you start work. If you're in any doubt, ask for a deposit. If you're in a lot of doubt, walk way or ask for the whole lot in advance. You can offer them a money-back guarantee if they're not happy, but this is your livelihood we're talking about. I got to a point where I realised that, often, our business, small though it was, was more financially robust and well established than the client's. In the Nineties dot.com boom I went to visit one prospective client. Their office was enormous, a whole floor of an achingly cool office building in Chelsea. One little detail set the alarm bells ringing though: no furniture. OK, another detail: no employees. So clearly, no sales. I asked for money upfront. I didn't get it. A month later they were gone, like a shiny digital soap bubble.

Whom to approach

The simple rule of thumb when pitching your copywriting services is that the smaller the client the bigger the job title. If you are approaching local firms, you are more likely to be talking to the managing director or possibly marketing director. If you are going after big industrial concerns, you're looking for a marketing manager of one stripe or another. Don't worry too much about precise job titles though, you can always ask for "the person responsible for your marketing". If you're targeting agencies, it will probably be the creative director or head of copy. Though again, if they're small, that might also be the managing director.

If you want to work for large companies and big-name brands, then in the absence of some fairly heavyweight contacts in your address book, you're probably going to be working through agencies. Smaller outfits will be more likely to hire you direct.

What if you don't have any contacts?

Everyone has contacts. It's just that some people's contacts are closer to the source of work than others. If you have a great contacts book – marketing managers from your industry, agency creative heads, whoever – you really want to work it hard, till the corners melt. Get to see every single person on your list. Don't be shy, don't be embarrassed and don't give up. Everyone will have one half-hour slot in their diary over the next three months, so make it yours. They will also, if they know you, want to help, even if that just means meeting you for a coffee.

If your contacts book is more at the friends and family level, work that too. Do any of your kids' parents run their own businesses? Does your sister-in-law handle marketing for a local events company? What about that nice couple you met

Everyone will have one half-hour slot in their diary over the next three months, so make it yours.

at your neighbour's drinks party? Didn't they say something about their video training business? Call them, email them or buttonhole them in the street and set up a meeting. Offer to buy them a coffee at the best deli in town. They'd be churlish to turn you down.

Or, pick out a list of 30 companies you really, really want to write for. Call their switchboard and say this:

Hello, I hope you can help me. [Asking for help will melt the heart of even the most steel-hearted receptionist, especially if you can make your voice sound a bit little-girl-lost (or little-boy-lost).

I need to write to the person who's in charge of marketing but I don't know their name. [If you ask for the name of the marketing manager you will often get the standard "we don't give out names, it's company policy" bum's rush.]

At this point the kindly lady (it's usually a lady) will either ask you whether you mean the marketing director or the head of branding or simply tell you what you need to know.

If they do give you the brush off, try this:

Of course, I totally understand it's company policy. But I have just set up my own copywriting company and I really need to make sure my letter gets through to the right person. [If you can suggest those big cartoon puppy-dog eyes in your voice I think they'll give in.]

If that fails, here is the black ops version. (And I apologise to all accounts departments for this – but it works, and when you have to put food on the table, it's an imposition you're willing to make, I think.)

You call the switchboard. They answer. You say this:

Accounts payable please. [Nobody screens calls for the finance department.]

Someone picks up. You say,

Oh, is that not marketing? Sorry, your switchboard put me through to the wrong department. Look, while I've got you, is your marketing manager still Liz Smith? [It never was, or maybe it actually was, but it doesn't matter. Because they will say…]

No it's Ken Thompson.

Or, surprisingly,

Yes, it's still Liz.

Ting! Thank them sweetly and get off the phone.

Or you can simply buy a list of email addresses or full addresses for marketing managers, HR directors or whoever else you want to pitch to and use that. Or join your local chamber of commerce or business association and get their membership directory. Though you need to be aware that making and storing a copy is a breach of their copyright. Or search on Google for "marketing <companyname>". We're straying into marketing tactics here so I'll hold off until Section 5.

How to build up your portfolio from scratch

Some copywriters make the move into freelancing from a marketing or agency background. They are lucky because they already have a portfolio. I did, and yes it helped. You may have one too, in which case you're starting higher up the ladder. But if you don't have a portfolio, because your last job was as a project manager, plasterer or full-time mum, don't worry. You already have a lot of the things clients are looking for: a copywriting business, the talent or skill to write copy, and the ability to understand how to turn your writing abilities into money for your clients. So you've never written copy in anger, who cares? Here are a few suggestions for getting your portfolio into some sort of reasonable shape.

You know that list of contacts you put together earlier on? Friends and relations, neighbours and local business owners? Get hold of them and offer to write some copy for them either free or for a fraction of your normal fee. Explain what you're up to and offer them the low price in exchange for a sample and a testimonial. Here's a sample email/letter you could use:

> *Dear Fran,*
>
> *I have just launched a new copywriting agency here in Newtown. I specialise in websites, particularly search engine optimisation.*
>
> *At the moment, because the business in its early days I am keen to build up a body of work for my portfolio. So I have a proposal for you.*
>
> *I'd like to offer you a rewrite of your home and about us pages for your website free of charge. In return, and if you're happy with what I produce for you, would you give me a testimonial and let me feature your website in my portfolio?*
>
> *To give you an idea of my abilities, here is a sample web page I wrote as part of my copywriting training. [link]*
>
> *I'll call you in the next couple of days to see what you think.*
>
> *Best regards,*
> *Andy Maslen*

Downside? You're working for nothing. Upside? You're building your portfolio. And because you are going to overdeliver (you are, believe me) you'll have a satisfied client who will be more likely to a) hire you for money next time, and b) recommend you to their contacts. If you're wondering what that "sample webpage" is, you've written a short webpage for a fictitious business (or maybe more than one) and posted it to your website on the portfolio page.

Another method is to take examples of advertising, emails or sales packs you've seen and rewrite them. Lay them out, or get a designer to do it for you, and post these to your website on, yes, your portfolio page. You need to delete any branding and make it clear that these are worked examples rather than paid jobs.

Or you could tell your client that although you don't currently have any examples of that particular sort of copy in your portfolio, you have recently written an article about it, then attach your latest blog post or e-zine article about it. They will see, rightly, that you're something of an authority and may just hire you on the spot.

Remember that if you're good at selling, you may get paying work without needing to show samples. I did on occasion. So you're getting paid and building your portfolio. Another freelance copywriter recently quoted a great phrase to me that she'd picked up at a seminar: "If you're doing it, you're qualified". In other words, have confidence in your skills and your clients will too.

If you're doing it, you're qualified. In other words, have confidence in your skills and your clients will too.

You may also find it easier to go after small jobs to begin with. Every business has communications where a full-service agency would be overkill – speaker biographies, staff handbooks, flyers, customer service emails. Offer to write those and you may find yourself under less pressure to demonstrate your record with examples of your work.

Or why not make contact with a few local marketing agencies. Be honest about where you are in your copywriting career, but wangle yourself an interview and offer to work for nothing if they'll let you loose on a couple of live projects. Providing you can demonstrate your abilities as a writer they might well go along with your proposal. After all, they get a competent copywriter taking on work, and they don't have to pay for it. (I suspect that only the most ethically challenged agency would pay you nothing. You might find you get to start building your portfolio and making a few quid.)

There are a number of websites – the so-called content mills – offering word rates for copywriters. Some as low as 2p a word. They are aimed primarily at delivering pages of content for websites with the aim of fooling Google into thinking they are relevant to users' searches. To me this isn't copywriting at all – more like typing. If you want to go for it, fine. Be aware though that this kind of stuff won't look that great in your portfolio and the money, frankly, is so poor you might as well go and work in a supermarket and write fiction in your lunch breaks. You'll make more money and write better stuff too.

What are direct clients looking for?

I call them *direct* clients because anyone who hires you is a client; I'm talking here about the companies whose products or services you're writing about, unmediated by any other agency. This is an easy one for me to answer, partly because I spent around ten years being a client, and partly because I've spent all my time since then working for direct clients.

Remember that the phrase "direct clients" covers every conceivable type of business. One-person bands, start-ups and internet entrepreneurs … small and medium sized enterprises (SMEs) … large national companies and multinationals … government departments … charities and non-governmental organisations (NGOs) … professional service firms such as lawyers, accountants and management consultancies … well, you get the picture I'm sure.

In an agency relationship, you will mostly be dealing with the head of copy or a creative director, plus maybe the account manager or director for the particular account you're working on, and an occasional client contact. With direct clients, it could be a marketing executive, manager or director, the MD, chairman or chief executive, head of fundraising, managing partner, HR manager ... almost anyone really. So you need to have a greater range of people skills if you're going to manage their expectations, sell your ideas, handle their revisions and deal with queries over your bill. They may want to offer you a risk-sharing deal (sometimes simply shorthand for not paying you unless or until the campaign makes any money). They may get fired before they've approved your copy, leaving a void you have to fill.

When I was a marketing director, I never hired freelance copywriters. Partly because we did it in-house, and partly because if there was any chance of the marketing department being overstretched, I would write it. (See the Introduction for where this behaviour got me.) But I did hire freelance designers, photographers and illustrators. I wanted them to "get" it. In other words, I wanted them to realise we were trying to shift merchandise. The end. Not to win awards. Not to prime their portfolios with interesting-looking brochures. Not to try out the latest ideas. Now I'm on the other side of the fence, this is still what 99 per cent of my clients expect. They want me to understand their business, the product I'm promoting, the aims of the campaign and, of course, the customer. I have to think like them.

Here's an exercise featuring a short and non-exhaustive list of what I think clients look for in a freelance copywriter. And once again, we won't put "excellent copywriter" on the list. If you weren't, they wouldn't even think of hiring you. Claiming you are one on your website makes you look, I feel, a little desperate. I've put all the things they look for, not just the reasonable ones. Maybe we can play a game where you put an R by the things you think are reasonable and a U by the things you think are unreasonable.

Exercise 3 – 25 client expectations

- Easy to get hold of in office hours.
- Willing to make changes to the copy.
- Friendly.
- Will work all night to meet a deadline.
- Does not charge extra for the above.
- Always meets or beats deadlines.
- Doesn't make additional charges over and above the original quote.
- Understands the client's industry and business.
- Accepts that the client's say is final.
- Prepared to haggle over fees.
- Can answer all their little grammar questions.
- Will come in for meetings whenever the client wants them.
- Does not charge for the above.
- Can offer advice on marketing as well as write copy.
- Does not charge for the above.
- Can recommend designers/photographers/printers/mailing houses.
- Does not charge for the above.
- Writes web copy AND optimises it for search engines.
- Does not charge for the above.
- Will work weekends.
- Does not charge extra for the above.
- Will discount fees on the promise of repeat business.
- Offers training in copywriting.
- Write more drafts than the original agreement.
- Does not charge extra for the above.

I'm guessing you spotted my little bit of fun.

Actually, clients have the right to expect anything from their freelance copywriter. And you can decide whether or not you're going to deliver. I may have already mentioned that I don't work evenings and weekends. Partly because I have other interests – I am interested in not being divorced for example – and partly because that's not when I'm most effective at writing copy. I also like to manage my time so it's not necessary. But that's not the point. The point is, what are *you* going to do? If you work evenings and weekends, fine. But let your client know at the outset that this is chargeable. Ditto all the other items in our list of expectations. In fact the best approach is to specify that they're chargeable, then, provided it doesn't disrupt your day, week or life too much, waive the fee and offer the extras free as a gesture of goodwill. You will become popular. Just make sure all those freebies aren't preventing you earning the money you want to.

There are other things clients are looking for too. They may want someone who offers some continuity. In large organisations, staff turnover can approach levels so high, anyone with two years' experience counts as an old lag. In those situations, a freelance who's been around for, say, five years, is a real asset. You can come to seem like a safe pair of hands and you can make this work to your advantage. Even having the odd anecdote about how things were before the last reorganisation can make you seem more experienced, more trustworthy and more likely to understand the current business. I say "seem", but in fact you are all those things. If you've been paying attention.

What are agencies looking for?

As my experience in this field is limited – to zero – I will simply quote from the responses given by the freelancers I interviewed for this book.

Richard Harrison: "Agencies tend to look for the ability to hit deadlines above all else, plus a can-do attitude that means they don't have to babysit you throughout a project. It's also handy if you can deal with all levels of client (from junior exec to boardroom)."

79

Relly Annett-Baker: "To have an understanding of their processes and requirements as well as their clients. But this isn't a hardship, it's fundamental to doing a good job. Research and process make up at least 50 per cent of my work. The writing is the easy bit!"

Peter Wise: "Nowadays, more than ever, agencies need someone with good writing skills. The interesting, conceptual stuff they're more likely to keep for themselves. Besides which, there are fewer genuinely creative agencies out there today. And where once a campaign might have been some press ads or posters, nowadays it could include direct mail, a microsite, html emails, a flyer and so on – all from the one agency. So a lot of copy.

"However, even if you're not the originator of the basic campaign idea, it helps if you have the ability and experience in conceptual work to be able to take someone else's idea, interpret it across different media and really make it sing. Although quite often you have to bite your tongue and work with a campaign idea that's actually pretty rubbish. You also need to be able to work with any designer/art director.

"Plus, you need to be like freelancers anywhere, flexible, ready to work at the drop of a hat and price yourself correctly."

Matt Ambrose: "What helped me get a foot in the door was my blogging expertise. I think agencies want freelancers who can add value to their service offering and who are full of ideas. In my case, initially I couldn't compete with freelancers with 20 years' direct mail experience so instead I differentiated myself by offering blog marketing expertise. My advice to other freelancers would be to think about what 'added value' services you can offer which make you more valuable to agencies and cover areas in which they might be lacking. Delivering on time and with the minimum supervision also go a long way."

Caroline Gibson: "Someone they can count on and who will deliver the goods."

Vince Love: "Andy, I find agencies are much more focused on the process of production than business clients are. Consequently a copywriter who submits good copy, on brief and on time is considered an asset, especially when the agency has to juggle all manner of issues to get a campaign out on schedule (which is most of the time). Conversely, if you don't get the brief by asking enough questions or turn your copy in late after several broken promises of doing so, you'll probably never hear from them (or their friends) again. As far as agencies are concerned, copy doesn't always need to change the world (although they love it when it does), but it must fit with the process they are committed to. I've also found that agencies, particularly smaller ones, often appreciate input based on expertise and experience. This can be a great value-add for a freelancer with some experience under his or her belt. Agencies also value a strong portfolio when first considering a writer – as opposed to business clients who can place more weight on the fact a writer seems to understand their business and be in tune with their target audience."

Sally Ormond: "The first thing to remember is that agencies will only take on copywriters with a track record, therefore for a newbie it can be hard to get a foot in the door.

"The agencies I work for have been very accommodating. I was upfront in telling them I wanted to work remotely with clients. This has certainly prevented me from getting some work, but there are plenty of companies out there who are happy to work remotely with copywriters. After all, with today's technology you can work from anywhere.

"Often deadlines are much tighter with agencies and you don't always get contact with the end client. At least that has been my experience to date. But other than that the process is pretty much the same."

Deadlines

The moment you win your first copywriting job, you encounter (or you should) the deadline. Deadlines will now be a fact of life for as long as you run your business. They are a contract term and, more importantly, a critical factor in establishing your reputation.

Far, far more important than how long something is going to take is when you're going to finish it. That's the deadline. And it's something you agree with the client. Now it may be that your client tells you when they need the copy by. In my experience, most clients are very reasonable and will specify a deadline that leaves you enough time to do the work. Others, though, will forget they need copy for, say, a new website until the last minute, then find a copywriter and expect then to write sparkling, optimised, punchy copy overnight.

One prospective client phoned me at 5.15 on a Friday afternoon and wanted to discuss copy for a new marketing campaign. When I asked when they needed it she said, "Monday morning". I didn't take the job.

You may not be averse to working evenings and weekends. But at any rate, and back to my original point, the deadline must be agreed. If the client stipulates a short deadline and you say "fine", that's still an agreement. But if you don't think you can deliver by that deadline, say so. Then you can either negotiate a more realistic deadline, or turn the job down.

As you become more established as a freelance it's likely you will always have a couple of jobs lined up after the current one finishes. So you need to let your client know when you can start, as well as when you can finish. I always say to people that I would rather they knew at the outset when I can deliver rather than saying yes to get the job then letting them down.

It's never a good idea to miss a deadline. You piss off your client and build the wrong kind of reputation. If circumstances mean you are going to miss a deadline, tell the client as soon as you can. Maybe there's a way round it, but there won't be if you simply keep quiet and deliver your copy late.

It's never a good idea to miss a deadline. You piss off your client and build the wrong kind of reputation.

SECTION 5
PRICING YOUR SERVICES

If you bill by the hour, you are probably putting an artificially low ceiling on your earnings.

If there's one single challenge that preoccupies freelance copywriters – freelance anythings, actually – it's pricing. There are a number of issues that influence how you price your copywriting services:

- Self-confidence/self-doubt
- Experience
- Reputation
- How much money you need
- How much money you want
- Salesmanship
- Poker skills

Before we get into the meat and potatoes of pricing (I will discuss all the options, though as you will see, I have my own views – quite strong ones – about the right way to do it), let's spend a few moments looking at each of these factors and how they affect pricing.

Self-confidence/self-doubt

I think it's fair to say that many freelance copywriters lack self-confidence. They might feel that because they're naturally good at writing they shouldn't also get well paid for it. "It's not as if I have to struggle with it." If they're new to the game, they may feel almost the reverse: that as they're still learning the craft, they don't deserve to be paid very much. Having interviewed nine female copywriters for this book, I am going to repeat the suggestion more than one of them made: that female copywriters tend to suffer from this problem more than their male counterparts. They shouldn't. But they do. If you're a woman reading this and you don't fit that profile, good! Note the irony here, that someone with a highly desirable skill lacks confidence <u>precisely because they possess it</u>.

Others, through commercial naiveté, imagine that if they ask for "too much", they'll simply get knocked back. The problem for these freelancers is they have no idea what "too much" is. Is £100 too much for a press release? Is £300 too much? Is it £500, £1,000 ... who knows?

Because we all start setting our prices when we're new to the game, we are all, to an extent, inexperienced. Those copywriters with an agency background have copywriting experience, but they have no more experience running their own copywriting business than an 18-year-old who just fancies having a crack at it. That means self-confidence is always going to be a challenge.

It's difficult to know how to address this, but here are a few thoughts. You have set up a copywriting business. You have trained, practised or otherwise honed your craft skills, so you can fairly say, to anyone who asks you what you do, "I am a freelance copywriter". Imagine two copywriters being asked that question. Copywriter one, Julie, has 25 years' experience. Copywriter two, Alfie, has two years' experience.

Interior: The Wordsmith Bar and Grill
Bartender: So, what do you do?
Julie: I'm a freelance copywriter.
Bartender: And you, what do you do?
Alfie: I'm a freelance copywriter.

The copywriters finish their drinks, pay up and leave.
Customer: Who were those two? I haven't seen them in here before.
Bartender: They're freelance copywriters.
Customer: Wow – I just read an article about copywriting. It pays really well. Hmmm, maybe I should be a copywriter.

See what I mean? If you lack confidence, then act like you have it to begin with because <u>nobody will know the difference</u>.

Experience

When you've been around a bit, you have the advantage that there's a steady flow of work, you have money in the bank and you're getting repeat business.

When you've been around a bit, you have the advantage that there's a steady flow of work, you have money in the bank and you're getting repeat business. This allows you to name your price and not collapse in a flood of salty tears if you get a rejection. You may also have solved the self-confidence problem by now. Read your testimonials. See how happy your clients are. You've also had the chance to experiment a little with pricing. Do that and you discover that what you thought was the most anyone would pay you for 200 words of web copy turns out to be very far from the truth. And you've had the chance to practise quoting prices – either on the phone, in person or in writing – and handling the response from the client. So now you're not imagining what people might say, you're drawing on memory of what they really say.

Reputation

If you have developed a reputation (a good one I mean, not because you always swear at clients who ask for revisions and then send them anonymous texts) as a copywriter, clients will come to you because you're you. Not just because you're a freelance copywriter. That means they want you in particular. And that means you have the scope, the liberty and the space to ask for more money. They will already be expecting this, because you are well regarded. If you wanted to hire an after-dinner speaker for a corporate event – a sports person, say – you would expect to pay more for this year's Wimbledon men's champion than the local golf pro. Now, the golf pro might be a hugely more entertaining speaker, but he doesn't have the reputation. So he can't command the same fee. It's called the law of supply and demand. There are lots of freelance copywriters: there's only one of you.

How much money you need

If you don't need much money, you may feel quite relaxed about pricing. As long as you can cover your modest outgoings and put a bit by for a rainy day – or for when you drop your laptop in a puddle on the way home from a client meeting – you're happy. Your motivation comes from self-fulfilment, your hobbies, wide social networks, voluntary work and collection of vintage typewriters. If, on the other hand, you have a swingeing mortgage payment to meet every month, three kids in private school and a serious designer label habit, you may feel that money is more of an issue. In both cases, your feelings about money will have an effect on your attitude to pricing. However, neither scenario is as critical in determining what you charge and your attitude to pricing as the next one.

How much money you want

Ah, now this is a bit more interesting. How much money do you want? Enough to pay the mortgage? Enough to pay off the mortgage? Enough to buy a new car? Enough to buy a new Aston Martin? Fifty thousand a year? A hundred and fifty? It's a good motivator however much you want. I have a friend who's a direct marketing consultant. In the early days of her consulting business, she stuck a Post It note on her office wall. Here's what's she'd written on it.

100 days @ £1,000/day

She wasn't making that. But that was the target. The aspiration. The dream. Every day she'd come into work and there it was. I think she's getting pretty close now.

When I resigned from my job as a marketing director, I had a financial target too. I wanted to make at least as much fee income in my first year as I had been paid in salary the year before. And just to be clear, this was what I wanted, not what I needed. I was fortunate enough to be earning more than I needed – I just couldn't face the idea of going backwards.

You see a lot of advertising on the web for copywriting courses promising you (or appearing to promise you) a six-figure income from freelance copywriting. They're usually in dollars but even so, that's a lot of money. For many people a six-figure income is a kind of Holy Grail. After all, once you're earning even £10,000 a year, you're on a five-figure salary, so the big six is the next target. And it's not unreasonable to aim to make £100,000 as a freelance copywriter. Why shouldn't you make that kind of money? Plumbers do. Dance teachers do. Marketing consultants do. (We'll talk more about six-figure copywriting in just a moment.)

Salesmanship

If you're good at selling you have an advantage when it comes to pricing. Why? Because you're good at showing customers the value of something. You know how to identify and read buying signals. You know how to counter objections. And you have an innate belief that what you're selling (copywriting) is going to transform their lives. So you're not shy about being well paid for it. The irony is that even copywriters who recognise that copywriting is about selling, not writing, aren't always so good at selling themselves. In person, I mean. Remotely, in writing, for clients, they're brilliant. Face-to-face or on the phone – on their own account – they fumble the ball, start talking about features (I can write SEO copy), not benefits (I can improve your Google PageRank), and crumple under pressure.

Poker skills

I'm not talking about bluffing here. I don't mean that when a client asks, "Have you ever written an HTML email before?" and you haven't, you say, "Yes, hundreds". I mean keeping a straight face and not blinking. Here's how it works.

You meet a prospective new client. The meeting goes swimmingly and then they ask the killer question:

> "So, what would you charge for that, then?"
> And you say, "I should think £300 would cover it."
> They look at you, but say nothing. You blink.
> "Er, but I could probably come down to £250."
> "Make it £200 and you've got yourself a deal."

Cutting your fee by a third is not the way to run a business. We'll discuss what to do instead later.

Getting to £100,000

Let's say, just for the sake of argument, your goal is to make £100,000 a year as a freelance copywriter. Actually no, not just for the sake of argument, because I think that's a perfectly reasonable income expectation for someone with your skills and abilities to make money for other people.

The single biggest mistake you can make...

Forgive me if you bill this way, and I know a lot of copywriters do, including some of the freelancers I interviewed for this book, but if you bill by the hour you are probably putting an artificially low ceiling on your earnings. If you do want £100,000 a year

89

you need to charge 2,000 hours at £50/hour. That works out as ten hours a day for 200 days. In other words, an insanely heavy workload that leaves you with no time to run your business or have much of a life outside work. Rare is the copywriter (or anybody else in a creative field) who can work productively for ten hours a day, every day, even assuming you can sell that many hours of your time. What if you double your hourly rate? OK, now you only have to sell 1,000 hours. But that's still five billable hours for 200 days a year. Or seven hours a day for 143 days. And I'm not sure you'll find that many clients or agencies willing to take you on at £100 an hour.

Because there's going to be a market rate for hourly-paid freelancers, you're going to find yourself trapped between the rock of a £50-an-hour rate and the hard place of the maximum number of billable hours you can sell or work in a year. Even if you don't want to earn £100,000 a year, you're at the mercy of an equation that everyone can see, that relates to input, not output. And that's the problem. When you bill by the hour, you're selling time. Like a factory worker. Or a shelf-stacker. Once you max out the hours you can work, your income is fixed at that time multiplied by your hourly rate.

But you're not selling time, or input. You're selling something hugely more valuable. Experience. Expertise. Talent. The ability to turn a company's fortunes around. To create an advertising campaign that will make them millions. To double their conversion rate. Output, in other words. That's valuable stuff. And it's worth paying for.

Ultimately, the way you charge for your services is up to you.

Ultimately, the way you charge for your services is up to you. It doesn't affect me. I think you're selling yourself short if you bill by the hour. So forgive me if I make my case further with an anecdote, a story, a thought experiment and a peek into your future.

First, the anecdote. Early on in my freelance career, I was talking to a more experienced writer and explaining that I felt unsure about asking for X amount of money for a job that was only going to take me a few hours. He said, "Well, Andy, think of it this way: it's three hours of typing and 12 years of R&D." In other words, the only reason you can do this job so quickly is because you've already spent so much time getting good.

Now the story. An old lady can hear a persistent, annoying drip from her bathroom tap every night, and it's keeping her awake. She calls a plumber. The plumber turns up at her house, looks at the dripping tap, then climbs into her loft. After a few seconds she hears three knocks on the pipe. The plumber climbs down from the loft and says, "That'll be fifty pounds and fifteen pence please". "How much?" she says. "For three knocks on a pipe! I need an itemised bill." So the plumber fishes the pencil from behind his ear and scribbles a few words on a piece of paper, which he presents to the old lady.

INVOICE
To knocking on pipe three times @ 5p per knock   15p
To knowing where to knock on pipe   £50
TOTAL   £50.15

Now the thought experiment. Suppose you currently take ten hours to write a four-page A4 brochure. You charge £50 an hour. So you bill £500. Excellent! On the way home one day, you trip on a loose paving slab, stumble over the curb and whack your head on a lamp-post. Once the miniature David Ogilvys have stopped flittering around your head, you pick up your stuff and carry on home. The next day you feel a little strange when you sit down to start your next assignment. It's a four-page A4 brochure. Somehow, you can think and write ten times quicker than you could yesterday. Instead of taking you ten hours, it takes you one. You send the copy to the client and wait. Within the hour they're on the phone, ecstatic. "This," they purr, "is fantastic. We're so happy we want you to write four more." So, my question to you is, what are you going to charge them?

91

According to your hourly rate you should put an invoice in for £50. I would say that looks unrealistic.

Finally, the crystal ball bit. It's ten years from now. Your business is thriving. And more to the point, you are hugely more experienced and practised than you are now. Even without the notional whack on the head, you are five times more productive than you used to be. So the job that used to take you ten hours now takes you two. Your hourly rate has gone up, of course. By 10 per cent a year. So it's now £130. But wait a minute. Now you're going to bill £260 for a brochure that's better by far than the one you wrote ten years ago and for which you invoiced £500. D'oh!

I guess the counter-argument to all of this is, "Yes, but I expect to be billing more hours in the future – so there'll be less down time and all my time will be billable so I will make more money than I do now". Well, good luck with that. Here's a newsflash. You will always have down time. It's a fact of life. If you don't, you're probably selling your services too cheap. It's called being a busy fool. In any case, do you really want to work more and more hours as you get older, just to boost your income? Wouldn't it be better to work fewer and fewer hours and still make more money?

Here's what I propose instead. (I only propose you think about it.)

...and what to do instead

I think you should charge by the project.

Doing it this way confers a number of advantages. For both you and your client. Your client gets a fixed price for the job that they can factor into their budget for the campaign or project overall. You sell it to them by explaining that if you have to wander about the park for eight hours waiting for inspiration to strike they don't have to pay you for it. That's down to you. And you? You get to make more money. Let me explain.

When you charge by the hour, is that actually what you're doing? To me, charging by the hour is an open-ended commitment from the client to pay you your hourly rate multiplied by the number of hours you take to finish the job. I suspect that very few clients – or copywriters – work that way. Charging by the hour tends to mean you quote based on your hourly rate, but give the client a maximum fee. Something like this:

My hourly rate is £50 and I think this job will take six hours, so my fee will be £300.

What happens after that is rarely good news for the copywriter who charges this way. If they're not very skilled at estimating how long things take, they end up spending more time on the job than they planned to, but are locked into the original fee. If they get the job done faster than they thought they would, some copywriters will charge the client less than the original quote.

If you charge by the hour and stick to the fee whether you are over or under your original time estimate, that looks to me suspiciously like a fixed fee for the project. The only difference is that by explicitly linking the fee to the number of hours worked, you are encouraging your client to think that they're paying for your time rather than your skill with words. And as we have already seen, the trouble with that approach is that the more skill you acquire over time, the less you will end up charging for the same job.

Remember also that when you charge by the project you are guaranteeing to the client that you will deliver standout copy: on brief, on brand and on time. They get what they hired you for – an ad, web-page, campaign or whatever, written to exemplary standards – regardless of how long it takes. A bit like a surgeon really. They charge by the operation (the private ones I mean) and just because it gets to half-past-four they don't just slope off to the pub leaving you with bits and bobs dangling all over the operating table.

For you, the advantages are clear. First, you establish in your client's mind that they are paying for output, not input. Value, if you prefer. Second, as your productivity increases, you make the same money for working fewer hours. Or more money for working the same number of hours. Third, you can take as little or as long as you like to finish a job because neither you nor the client is watching the clock. You do, still, have to write to deadline, which we covered at the end of Section 4.

Ultimately, there will always be a minimum time you will need for any job, but as you become more experienced, that experience will produce better copy and hopefully better results for your client – in less time. Experience isn't tangible, it isn't measurable and it's hard to put a price on it – but it is valuable. And that's what your client is paying for.

Maybe, if you work with agencies more than direct clients, the day-rate is still where it's at. Never having done it I can't comment. Although I think it would be worth a discussion next time an agency asks you your rates. But for your direct clients, I really think it's worth making the switch.

OK, let's assume that you are going to start charging by the project. The big question is, how much?

Where do you pitch your prices?

To give you an idea of the current going rate for freelance copywriters, I surveyed my interviewees. But these are only hourly/daily rates (and you know by now my thoughts on that way of charging for your services). Nevertheless, here's what they said. (I have averaged their answers.) Remember that not all of them charge for their own services by the hour: these are what they know about rates in their area or industry.

	Per hour	Per day
No experience:	£23	£175
5 years' experience:	£39	£300
10 years' experience:	£55	£400+

A couple of my interviewees commented that there has been little or no upward movement in these rates for <u>ten years</u>.

I also came across the following table on the Major Players Recruitment website:

ART DIRECTORS, COPYWRITERS & TEAMS	PERM (£K)	FREELANCE PER DAY
Graduates	18-21	min wage
Junior	20-30	150
Midweight	32-45	250
Senior	50-65	300-350
Group Head	50-70	300-350
Head of Copy/Art	50-70	300-350
Deputy Creative Director	60-80	300-350
Creative Director	70-120	350-400
Exec Creative Director	120+	400+

© Major Players Recruitment

Rather than subject these figures to a detailed critical analysis, I will just draw your attention to two values: the first and final in the freelance day rates column. My interpretation of the first is that you are better off gaining some experience – any experience – before embarking on a career as a freelance copywriter. And of the second, that if you divide the day rate into the equivalent salary, you can see how unrealistic is any expectation of salary-matching while charging by the day.

Here are some further observations on rates from my interviewees:

Tom Albrighton: "In my view, £300–£400 a day is realistic and reasonable for 5-10 years' experience. It will deliver a good salary based on a reasonable number of days worked per year (i.e. allowing holidays), leaving time for admin tasks and generating enough to cover business costs such as computers, phone and accountancy (often forgotten by outsiders evaluating freelance fees).

"It's also important that the fee reflects the value obtained by the client, insofar as this is possible. For example, a copywriter might spend half a day writing a company descriptor that gets used on website home pages, presentations, white papers, blogs, introduction letters, brochures and elsewhere – shaping first impressions of the company for years and years. In my view, that's easily worth £150 – probably closer to £1,500, but there you go!"

Claire McCarthy: "If you're working for agencies/third parties they will always demand a better rate, usually 15-20% discount. From what I've learnt, small businesses simply aren't prepared to pay the higher rates for copywriting, and always go for the cheaper option, even if they realise they may not get the best results. For example, if they are getting a website designed, they may only be paying around £300-£500 for the website itself, and simply don't understand how copy can easily cost just as much – they see it as very much a secondary concern, rather than of equal or greater importance to design. As we discussed on the phone, copywriters do their best to explain the value of good copy but often the lower rate wins out in the end. Larger businesses, in my experience, are usually prepared to pay much more."

Jill Tomlinson: "I don't know what a starting rate is these days for a new freelancer. The content farms and 'bid for jobs' set-ups have also skewed the pitch for newcomers. For established people, it depends where you are in the country and what your skills are. People will pay for good writers and will understand that good copy is preceded by careful research and preparation. That takes time."

Matt Ambrose: "*The Guardian* recently ran a forum on copywriting. Somebody posted a question on rates saying they were about to go freelance on the back of a number of years' (I think it was seven) experience and were going to charge £40/hour, which got a thumbs up from the panel."

Peter Wise: "That's an interesting one. I think a freelance copywriter with no experience will struggle to get £200 a day. Five years should be OK for £300. In mainstream DM/digital agencies, the price seems to have been more or less static for several years now, for those with ten or more years' experience, at between £300 and £400, talking to my freelance friends (I hardly do any work for agencies nowadays). A few may get more. Very few I know charge by the hour. What also seems to be different is that very few are doing long stretches – mostly just a week or two. When I started out freelance, I worked for one agency almost full-time for over two years, albeit at slightly below market rate, and did several other stints of several months each.

"Direct clients, it depends on whether they have a marketing budget or not! Of course, one of the advantages of working mostly from home is that a 'day' is a flexible concept in some cases – and also often cuts out two hours of commuting."

Sarah Turner: "I have to say, at a local level (Kingston, Wimbledon BNI, Best of, Athena etc.) most copywriters are charging the same, irrespective of experience or expertise. I do know that clients think a copywriter's fee should always be less than the designer's. (Why I don't know.) Some designers I work with charge only £65 an hour. (And that's an agency rate.)"

Richard Harrison: "A tricky one that depends on the client as much as anything else. But… No experience – it will be hard to convince anyone to pay you anything at first. Once a company gives you a chance (based on your portfolio, or the fact that you're offering your services for free), you might then be able to charge £25/hour or £150/day on future projects. (The day rate doesn't usually stack up to 8x the hourly rate.) Five years – £250-£350/day (You can charge more because having more experience means you'll take less time to do a given project and you'll have to do fewer revisions.) Ten years – £500+ a day. You should be an expert in your field by now. However, market conditions can make some clients flinch at such fees."

Caroline Hampstead: "I was talking to a lawyer who had used a copywriter (not me) for some work, and the lawyer was saying what a good job she did and how surprised she was at how little she charged (which to me means she'd have happily paid quite a bit more). I think a lot of copywriters undervalue themselves, and if your client charges themselves out at hundreds of pounds an hour, they probably won't mind paying you well if you do a good job."

So there you are. If you're charging for your time, try pitching your rates around those benchmarks. Bear in mind that agencies will expect a discount – maybe as much as 20 per cent. Let's put them into context first though. About once every six weeks a scruffy blond surf dude turns up at our door and cleans our windows. He charges £15 and takes about 20 minutes. That means his hourly rate, allowing for walking next door, is about £40. If he cleans the windows of 24 houses in a day, he makes £360. That is to say, more than a middleweight freelance copywriter. He also gets to work in the sunshine, gets paid in cash immediately and doesn't have to attend meetings or have clients query the way he works.

But what about my way of charging? By the project. Rather than offer you my rates, I want to encourage you to set your own. You'll want to bear in mind a number of factors:

- Your experience
- Whether you have any specialist expertise
- Your reputation (if you have one) – in your city/region/industry/specialism
- Your poker skills (see the beginning of this section)
- How much you think your client will pay

When I started out, I based my project fees on a nominal hourly rate that was itself based on the salary I had just left behind. But as I raised my rates that link became tenuous, then non-existent. Now I have a rate-card that I consult whenever a client asks me for a quote. It's based on how much I have charged in the past and what I know about how much clients are willing to pay for different kinds of project. For example, projects that link directly to revenue – direct mail letters or emails, for example – tend to command higher fees than internal documents, press releases and exhibition materials.

You might base your fees on a combination of factors, including how long a reasonably efficient copywriter might take (but you aim to be better-than-averagely efficient); the value the client places on the project; whether they need it in a hurry; and the word count. I don't make an explicit charge per word, but I would charge more for a 1,000-word sales letter than a 500-word sales letter. Having said that, I always say I don't charge for typing, I charge for thinking, and you have to think just as hard to write a short letter as a long one. Maybe harder, as it's tougher to isolate the killer sales points when you are also trying to stay within a tight word limit. In a quote sometimes attributed to Mark Twain (though also to Blaise Pascal and Doctor Johnson), he apologised to a friend with the line, "I'm sorry I wrote you a long letter; I didn't have time to write you a short one".

Want some example prices? How about these for a copywriter with a couple of years' experience...

- A press release   £200-300
- A short sales email/letter   £400-650
- A long sales email/letter   £750-1,000
- A press ad   £400-650
- A brochure   £100-200 per page
                                              depending on copy density
- A website   £100-200 per page depending
                                              on length of copy

Ultimately, you want to aim to charge what the market will bear. I always understood this because in my corporate career we were selling publications with a physical value of about £20 for anything up to £5,000. The value wasn't the paper, toner and binder, it was the market intelligence and insights they contained. Sound familiar at all? Ideally, you would be charging a penny less than the figure your client would reject. Trouble is you don't know what that number is, and they, if they have any sense, will never tell you. So you test. If, over the course of the next six months you are going to be asked to quote to write, say, 20 websites, brochures or letters, try out a few different prices. If you win them all you're pitching your prices too low. If you lose them all, too high. If you lose a quarter to a third, I'd say you have it about right. But remember this: if you doubled your prices and lost 50 per cent of your work you'd be ahead of the game. Now you're making just as much money as you were before, but in half the time. And if you lose 49 per cent of your work you're better off financially too.

Are you giving it away?

A common mistake – and one I freely admit to making myself from time to time – is giving it away.

A common mistake – and one I freely admit to making myself from time to time – is giving it away. Not necessarily copy, but advice, recommendations or "tweaks" to copy a client has drafted. It's the first of these that can cripple your profitability. Typically, you get drawn into a long conversation on the phone with a potential client (or, occasionally, a current one) about the tactics they should employ, the approach to search engine optimisation (SEO) they should adopt, what you think is working for your other clients and so on. There's a name for the service you're providing on these calls. It's called consultancy. Other kinds of self-employed professionals charge – handsomely – for it. I would say a marketing consultant advising a client on marketing should be charging anywhere from £500 to £2000 a day. So the next time you spend an hour on the phone idly chatting with a client you've never met before and who has never offered you a penny, remember you're leaving money on the table.

You could argue that you have to do a bit of this sort of thing to demonstrate your credentials and close the sale. And you're right. You do have to do a bit of it. But speaking only from my own experience, there have been times when I made the transition from demonstrating my credentials to giving free advice. Be alert to the possibility that you might be giving it away and politely suggest to the persons on the other end of the phone that this is something you could definitely help them with, and it falls under your copy advisory service, for which you charge £50 an hour.

Ballparks, estimates, and quotes

When a client asks you what you would charge them to write a piece of copy, there are three ways to give them a price. First, you can give them a ballpark figure. You should always try to give a ballpark figure as a range: "For a press release I normally charge £200-£300". This allows you to test the client's reaction and decide whether their expectations are in line with your fees. If they faint, slam the phone down or say "HOW much?" you can probably assume you won't be working together. You have also saved yourself the time of preparing a formal quotation.

Second you can give them an estimate. This tends to be a single figure but isn't binding. You provide an estimate with a line like this:

"For a 200-word press release based on an interview with you on the phone, it would be around £250. If you can give me a written brief by email I can send you a formal quote by return." This is your chance to start closing the sale. You need to establish a couple of details before you quote, but your final

101

price is probably going to be £250 plus or minus a bit. So what are these details? Here are four things I like to get straight with a client before quoting:

- When they want it.
- How many people will be involved in approving the copy.
- The seniority of the people approving the copy.
- Whether they will also be approving the brief.

Third, you give them a formal quotation. It doesn't have to be a long document, but it does state what you will do, by when, and how much you will charge them. An email quotation could simply say:

Dear Chris,

Good to talk just now. Based on our conversation, I understand you want me to write a 250-word press release on the new launch of your service. I will interview you on the phone rather than visiting your offices, and will submit the first draft and subsequent drafts as Word documents.

My fee will be £275 + VAT.

I can deliver the first draft by [time and date].

Please let me know by email if you would like to go ahead.

Kind regards,
Andy

Remember that your quote is also an opportunity to close the sale.

Remember that your quote (or quotation – I use the terms interchangeably) is also an opportunity to close the sale. Don't make the mistake of assuming all you have to do is quote the fee. Maybe you include a summary of your credentials or experience in press-release writing. Maybe you reference a couple of recent clients. Maybe you explain what they can expect as results (though you must be careful not to promise results). Whatever you do, make sure your quote is a mini-sales pitch. Because apart from anything else, your client/prospective client may not be the only person involved in the buying decision, and may forward your email to their colleagues. A bald, one-line statement of your fees may not impress someone who hasn't spent 20 minutes on the phone being swayed by your smooth presentation of your skills and credentials.

Discounting

I'm not sure, but I reckon that if your client were to book the world's most bankable female pop star for a private birthday bash and asked for a discount, they'd get a fairly swift and unequivocal response from her people. No surprise there really, is there? There's only one of her, after all. I suspect that your client wouldn't even get as far as asking for a discount.

So why is it that they cheerfully ask you for a quote and then immediately start asking for a discount? "Because there are loads of copywriters out there who will work for less," you answer. "And if I don't discount they'll go elsewhere." But just like our pop star, there is only one you. Sure there are other copywriters, but your client hasn't gone to them, they've come to you. So they must want you. Which means you shouldn't bend over the moment they ask you to "sharpen your pencil" or whatever phrase they employ to put you on the back foot.

Marketing budgets are often under pressure, especially if the company's just posted some less-than-stellar results, and this makes self-employed copywriters feel nervous. If the client genuinely has less money than last year and has genuinely had their budget cut then you will have to find a way to accommodate them – or lose the work. But all this could also simply be cover for those savvy purchasers of copywriting services who always ask for – and expect to get – a discount. Now they have an extra lever to pull…

"Oh well, Jim, we know that's your normal fee but you see what with these budget cuts and all we just don't have £500. If you can do it for £400, you have yourself a deal."

Don't give in automatically. Instead have a think. This is a buying signal. They want you to write their copy. Here's what you can do instead. Start negotiating.

Suppose they're the hard-nosed type and simply challenge you on price, saying it sounds too high. You could bat it right back at them by saying, "Oh, compared to what? What sort of figure did you have in mind?" Now the boot's on the other foot. Either they admit they don't have the faintest idea, in which case you are in a strong position to hold the line. Or they tell you their budget. Which you can settle for or reject as you wish.

In response to the question above, you could say, "OK, look, I understand where you're coming from but honestly? I can't cut my rates by 20 per cent just like that. Can we agree that I'll do one draft and one set of revisions? That's going to save me work and I can offer you a reduction."

Or you can ask them for money upfront. Cash flow is important however long you've been in business, so you might feel able to offer a discount for advance payment. I'd say five to ten per cent wouldn't be unreasonable.

Or try to turn a one-off job into a bulk deal. If your client wants you to write a press release, ask them how many they expect to send out this year. Offer them a deal where they commission a bunch of press releases now and you offer them a discount. Just be careful that you don't start discounting immediately. That series could soon turn into two, or even the original one, which you have now written for less than you meant to. Instead, follow the advice of my accountant, who told me, "Don't discount on the promise of a deal, discount on the delivery". In plain terms, calculate the cash discount for the series of press releases, but cut it all from the back end of the series. So you do the first few at full price, the next one at half price and the final one for nothing. Or however the figures work out. Now your client gets the full amount of discount, but only once they have delivered on the deal by commissioning the whole series of press releases.

This is all lovely when the work is flowing in and your confidence levels are high. You know you can afford to turn away clients without the cash because there are plenty more queuing up to hire you. In leaner times, clearly, the temptation to discount is much higher. We aren't immune at Sunfish, though we always make sure we trade concessions for discount. This is the difference between haggling (which we never do) and negotiating (which we do a fair amount of the time).

Haggling is simply firing numbers at each other, one from a low point, one from a high point, and waiting till you reach some point in the middle where you both agree to deal. The souk, in other words. Negotiating is a process of trading concessions, some, but not all of which may be financial. For me, things I am prepared to negotiate are deadlines, the number of drafts, the number of design proofs, payment terms, whether the client will agree to do a video testimonial, the length of copy and, yes, the fee.

There are also soft factors that may lead you to discount. Is the product of personal interest to you? We did a lot of copywriting for the BBC's *Top Gear* magazine a few years ago. I was so pleased I would probably have written it for nothing (I didn't tell the client that – sorry Lou.). Do you share a philosophical or ethical position with your client? If you do work for a charity, you may discount because you believe in what they're trying to achieve. In a sense this isn't discount-for-nothing, because you're tapping into what psychologists call warm-glow altruism. You get a good feeling about yourself and your client gets a discount. Do you believe working for this particular client will open doors? A so-called reference account? That halo effect is worth paying for. Are you just starting out as a freelance copywriter? Will the client give you a nice testimonial and, more to the point, let a newbie loose on their marketing campaign? Yes? Then that's worth mucho discount.

So the takeaway message from this section is, discount if you must, but try to make sure the client gives up something in return.

Price-quote confidence booster

When I was preparing this section, I spoke to a young copywriter about making the switch from charging by the day to charging by the project. I gave her a one-man role-play to show what I'd say when quoting for a job and meeting resistance from a client.

"I wish I was as good as you at selling on the phone," she said. "But I just don't have the confidence".

That's a pretty common problem – or let's call it a challenge – so here's an exercise you can try to give yourself a confidence boost.

Exercise 4 – gaining confidence in quoting prices
- Step 1 Find a mirror – a bathroom mirror is ideal. Pick a project you currently quote for at, say £200. Say the following out loud:
  "For [project type] I normally charge £200."
- Step 2 Now add £50. And repeat...
  "For [project type] I normally charge £250."
  If you blink or see yourself look away or fidget, say it again. And keep saying it until it sounds about as controversial as telling them your name.
- Step 3 Now add another £50. And repeat...
  "For [project type] I normally charge £300."
  If you blink or swallow nervously, stammer or flub your line, repeat Step 2.
- Step 4 Take off the extra £100. Asking for £200 now seems like you're underpricing, making it easier for you to have confidence in the value of what you're offering and hold the line with discount-savvy clients.

SECTION 6
WHAT IS A MARKETING STRATEGY, AND DO YOU REALLY NEED ONE?

I suggest you spend at least 20 per cent of your time on marketing.

Want to be a successful freelance copywriter? Even more important than getting your pricing right is getting your marketing right. Because without clients your fees can be anywhere and you'll still be eating food out of skips. It's better to be a low-priced copywriter with lots of clients than a premium-priced copywriter with none. This section is all about the channels and methods you can use to promote your business. Actually, let's stop pussyfooting around with words like"marketing" and "promote". You have to be able to sell. I called my first copywriting book *Write to Sell*, because that's what it's all about. Now you have to apply to your own business the same ideas you apply to your clients' businesses.

It sounds great when you're just starting out. You know…

Life partner:	What are your doing, love?
You:	I'm working on my marketing strategy.
Life partner:	That's nice. By the way, here's the gas bill. Oh, and our mortgage just went up by £150 a month.
You:	Oh, OK. Maybe I'd better start calling a few people.

A marketing strategy should be a document or an idea that says how you intend to win business.

A marketing strategy should be a document or an idea that says how you intend to win business. It's a rule for making decisions about marketing. You might make a strategic decision to build a reputation as an SEO guru. That will lead you to invest time and money in tactics that reinforce that position. You will want to start an SEO blog, contribute to SEO forums, write articles about SEO and optimise your website for keywords like SEO copywriting.

Equally, you might decide that your strategy is based on networking, because you're good with people face-to-face. So you join things: your chamber of commerce, local networking clubs, societies and associations. If there's a chance to get in front of people, perhaps at a conference, you go for it.

Here's a strategy recommendation for you. I suggest you spend at least 20 per cent of your time on marketing. If you work a five-day week, spend a day a week thinking about how you're going to win more clients. Not just thinking of course: writing, blogging, networking, writing AdWords, calling contacts, whatever it is you do to put money in the bank. Do it all the time, too. The temptation is to leave sales and marketing until you have a quiet spell. But then it's too late. Virtually nothing you can do this week will bring in work this week. With the possible exception of cold calling. Which none of us likes doing. At all. So we don't. So you keep selling and marketing all year round, even when you're busy. They call it mending the roof when the sun's shining. Given that we're also supposed to be making hay while the sun shines I don't know quite how you fit it all in, but fit it in you must.

To the question, do you need a marketing strategy, I think the answer is a simple no. You can get by without a marketing strategy and rely instead on good, old-fashioned activity. Make one call every day. Write one blog post every week. Tweet twice a day. Attend one networking meeting a month. This is not a strategy, but it will probably bring in work. And that's worth a heck of a lot more than any strategy. I give you the following story as an example. Two friends of mine were discussing whether to set up in business together. Jeff and I were having a drink one day and he said, "I see my role as handling strategy. I'm going to figure out where we should be going and what we should be doing". I said, "Who's going to do the selling, then?" "Oh, Helen's going to handle that side of things". This type of thinking is fatal. And in fact they never did start that company. If you're working for yourself you don't have the luxury of being a strategist. Strategy is one of the biggest displacement activities I can think of. Even large companies aren't immune. They're the biggest offenders. But they have the money to employ strategic people to think strategic thoughts. But for us? With our one or two-man bands? Forget it. Concentrate instead on those activities – tactics if you prefer – that you feel comfortable with and which you feel will likely lead to more work. Test and refine them by all means. Add in new ones and ditch the unproductive or uninteresting. If it helps, write a few notes that summarise your marketing and sales approach.

Mine, which I have pursued relentlessly from day one, was what I grandly titled the guru strategy. It read, in full, "books, articles, speeches, training". I intended to build a reputation as an expert and those were the means I would use. Since then I have expanded it to include e-zines and a couple of other channels, but the underlying idea remains unchanged.

Literature

A long time ago, when I was an anthropology student at university, I mistakenly stumbled into a lecture on English literature. By the time I realised my mistake the thing had started and I was too embarrassed to stand up and walk out. The learned academic type delivering the lecture peered over his half-moon spectacles and addressed us all: "What," he asked, "do we mean by literature?". He meant fine writing. I mean brochures, flyers, posters and other bits of paper or card you use to promote your copywriting business. The question is, do you need literature?

And the answer is, no you don't. About six months after we launched Sunfish I decided we "needed" a brochure. I spent ages writing the copy, got it designed and then asked a printer I knew to do me a thousand. Three years later, when the brochure was out of date and we still had 950 left, I pulped them. I've never repeated that mistake. Of course, the web means you don't need a brochure, but sometimes a little postcard or flyer can be helpful at networking meetings or even as a leave-behind after a client meeting.

Promotion channels – picking the ones that work for you

The good news (or is it?) if you're starting a copywriting business today is that you have many more channels to promote your services than I did when I started out in the mid-Nineties. The biggest difference is social networking and blogging. Actually, we did have social networking back then. We called it going to the pub. In this section I want to take a look at each of the main promotional channels you can use. I won't go into exhaustive detail, partly because there are lots of specialist blogs and books you can find to do that better than I can, and partly because if I attempted it, we'd end up with a book the size of a house brick. You wouldn't want to read it, and believe me, I wouldn't want to write it.

What I will do is offer you my thoughts on their strengths and weaknesses, how you could exploit them effectively, how they tie together and, where they're channels I use myself, share examples of the copy or approach I use. I have ranked them in order of money they've brought into our agency. This is as much a reflection of my preferences and background as the effectiveness of each channel in itself. What works for us may not work for you.

Word of mouth/referrals

This isn't the first channel I used. For the obvious reason that when you don't have any clients it's hard to get people talking about you and referring their colleagues to you. But over the years it has consistently been the channel that has brought in the most business. And not just business, but the *right* kind of business. I can give you a quick pen portrait of the ideal Sunfish client. She's a marketing manager of a medium-to-large information company. Like any industry, the information business is very incestuous, with people moving between the major players. They tend to know one another, and when they need outside help they turn, not to Google, but to their contacts.

One of the great advantages of word of mouth is... well, what do you think it is? In fact, why don't you write down all the reasons you can think of to invest in building word of mouth in the spaces below.

_____

_____

_____

_____

_____

_____

_____

_____

If you said, because it's free, give yourself a star. If you said, because you have to spend less time convincing each new client you know what you're talking about, give yourself another star.

Word of mouth is so valuable because your existing clients are doing the selling for you.

Word of mouth is so valuable because your existing clients are doing the selling for you. They get asked "Hey Fred, do you know anyone who's any good at SEO copywriting?" and they say, "Yes, give this guy a call. We used him and he's excellent."

Now when you get the call, the client is already pretty sure you're up to the job because someone they know and trust just told them you are. All you have to do is not blow it.

So is word of mouth really free? Well, almost. Certainly there's no money involved. All you have to do is be very, very, very good at what you do. Offer extra help and advice (but see my points in the section on pricing). Be easy to deal with and flexible. Always meet your deadlines. Better yet, come inside them. But there is another thing you can do to build word of mouth. It works the moment you get your first client. Ready?

You ask your clients to talk about you to their friends and business colleagues. That's right, ask for what you want. Maybe something like this would work:

Hi Jean,

Really glad you liked the web copy. I'm sure that was in part due to the brief you gave me. Nothing left out, which is a rarity these days!

I'm just wondering if you could do me a favour. I'm pretty busy at the moment but I'm also looking for more clients in your industry.

Would you be able to recommend me to your contacts? Obviously it's up to them whether they use me – or even call (!) – but it would be really helpful if you could point them my way.

Hope you can help.

Best wishes,
Sam

Word of mouth is such a no-brainer that it must be part of your promotional armoury. To a certain extent it just happens, whether you push it along it or not. And that's why it has to come with a little health warning for your business. Clients will talk about all suppliers, not just the good ones. I suspect that they will talk more about the bad ones than the good ones. After all, when you get good service in a shop, it might make you smile, but because it's what you expect you don't go home and blog about it or regale your friends with the story in the pub. But when you get dumped on from a great height, that's the story you share. It's human nature.

I remember being told on a marketing course that on average, people will tell three others about a positive experience they've had, and nine about a negative one. What I'm leading up to is this: if you screw up, or get arsey with a client, the word of mouth keeps working. Only now you get a reputation for being incompetent or difficult. Doesn't matter whose fault it was, you get the flak. So be polite, bite your tongue when they want that 11th draft and roll with the punches. You will win in the long run.

PR

One of the jobs we all get asked to do now and again is to write a press release. The basic rule is to tell the reader, in the opening paragraph, the who, what, where, when and why of the story.* But we can use them too, to promote our own businesses.

As cost-free advertising goes, the humble press release has little to touch it. Even Google AdWords start to look expensive in comparison. And your story can be pretty soft news. The launch of your copywriting business is a genuine news story for your local paper. If you have a background in a particular industry, maybe the trade journal or magazine will run a short piece about your move from the corporate world to freelance.

One of my first marketing efforts was to send out a short press release to a fairly esoteric industry newsletter called *Business Information Review* – one of the house journals for the bit of the publishing industry I was working in. The editor was a friend of mine and we had attended the same conferences for years. So it was a natural move to send Pam a press release. One of the people who read that issue was Anthony Ray, who at that time was the Research Director for The Economist Group, publishers of *The Economist* newspaper (Anthony now runs his

---

For a more detailed discussion of press release copywriting, please see Chapter Four of The Copywriting Sourcebook, *also by Andy Maslen.*

own business specialising in market research for the publishing industry).

One of the Group's businesses was the Economist Intelligence Unit, and they were one of the companies I had decided I wanted to work for. Anthony asked me to go in for a meeting to discuss selling to libraries – a market I had been involved in for several years in my corporate marketing job. Nothing came from that meeting directly, but he did later pass on my details to a colleague in the marketing department. They in turn asked me to go in to talk about direct marketing, and from that meeting was spawned a relationship with the company that still exists today. Over the years, we have worked on hundreds of projects for The Economist Group, from direct mail promotions for conferences to website copy to editing staff handbooks and running copywriting workshops. Not bad for a single 250-word press release.

Try to issue regular releases, to the print media in the sectors you focus on, to your local press and to the web (including your own website). It's all good background publicity. And write about everything. Just won a new account? Write a press release. Had a client's website go live? Write a press release. Had an article published? Write a press release.

E-zine

E-zine is still, I think, a term of art within the internet marketing community. I suspect most clients and recipients call them newsletters or e-newsletters. Doesn't matter.

I launched our monthly e-zine in October 2001. It's been a consistently good source of leads and out-and-out paying gigs. Some very good clients have only ever come to us via the e-zine. For a copywriter, writing and distributing an e-zine should be easy, if not mandatory. You're a writer, so writing it should be effortless – something not true for many self-employed professionals. It gives you a chance to position yourself as an expert in your chosen field – SEO, direct marketing, corporate publicity, whatever – and, most important of all, it gives you permission to remind your list that you exist as often as you send it out. On which subject, I would recommend you send out your e-zine at least monthly. Less than that and you risk missing the times when your recipient is in the mood for opening it and you also fail to establish it as a task you have to complete each month or fortnight or week.

The trick to creating a successful e-zine is really no trick at all. You have to write something your readers find either useful or entertaining.

The trick to creating a successful e-zine is really no trick at all. You have to write something your readers find either useful or entertaining. Or preferably a combination of the two. We all subscribe to e-zines, probably too many, perhaps lured by the freebies on offer. Then when they start arriving in our inboxes, we're back to that feeling of busyness and delete them unread. So for yours to get opened and clicked through you do have to work hard at the content. But given that each issue should be fairly short (400-500 words is ideal), you don't have to sweat buckets writing them. Subject ideas could include the following:

- Top tips
- A book review
- A list of useful websites or blogs
- An opinion piece about a particular form of copywriting
- A case study
- An interview
- Some research you've come across on the web
- A how-to article

The bigger question is, how are you going to build your list. Initially, you can try punting out your e-zine to all your email contacts. Just make sure you avoid the spammer label by explaining this is a one-off mailing because you think they'll be interested.

Then offer them the chance to opt in and explain you won't send them any more issues until and unless they explicitly ask you to. In the e-zine business, it's all about opt-in, and disregarding this principle will land you in all sorts of trouble. You could try an accompanying note that reads something like this:

Dear Fred,

I have just launched my e-zine – Jean's Copy Tips and I thought you might like to see the very first issue.

This one is all about SEO tips for bloggers. I intend to cover a different SEO issue every month with loads of practical advice and tips on getting it right.

I hope you enjoy reading it but because I know your time is precious, I won't bombard you with future issues if you don't want them.

Here's my suggestion. If you'd like to join the list and receive a new issue every month, please email me with a simple "sign me up" message. If not, do nothing and I promise I'll leave you in peace!

Looking forward to hearing from you,

Best regards,
Jean

In each issue, make sure you include a message asking the recipient to pass it on to their friends and colleagues. And get your designer (if you use one) to embed a little form to make it easy for them to forward it.

You should also make sure you have a prominent sign-up form on your website – on every page – and have a link to a dedicated sign-up page in your email signature. I have really seen the value of our e-zine, to the extent that getting people to sign up is the main purpose of the Sunfish website. On which subject...

Website

Do you need a web presence if you're a freelance copywriter? Yes. Do you need a website? Er, depends what you mean. I set up our first website at pretty much the same time as the business itself. My brother-in-law did it for us. Then, a few years later I did a contra deal and swapped some copywriting with a web design company for a redesign of our site. A few years later still I took their site apart, kept the graphics and redesigned the site myself using a simple web design program called Namo WebEditor. Are you beginning to see a pattern here? That lasted until 2010 when I finally bit the bullet and actually paid some money to a professional to give us a refresh.

Now we finally have a site that looks great (to my eyes, at least) and does all the things I want it to. The code complies with the guidelines set out by the World Wide Web Consortium (W3C) so it should be more attractive to search engines (although we have always had top rankings for the key words and phrases that interest us).

But, as an experiment, I stopped writing this section and set up a simple blog on WordPress.com: it took me exactly five minutes. It's not very big and it's not particularly clever, but it is there and it does work. And it cost me precisely nothing.

Like any piece of marketing copy or element of a campaign, your website needs to have a clearly defined purpose.

Like any piece of marketing copy or element of a campaign, your website needs to have a clearly defined purpose. Is it to attract new clients? (In which case search will form a very important part of your strategy for your site.) Is it a credentials piece so people you've already made contact with can check you out? (In which case you'll need lots of testimonials and examples of your work, plus a client list.) Is it to drive subscriptions to your e-zine? (In which case you'll need a well thought out sign-up box on every page.) Is it to build your personal brand as some sort of communications expert or copywriting guru? (In which case you'll want lots of articles and downloads demonstrating your knowledge.)

Most likely it will be a bit of all of those, but I think it works best when you assign each of these priorities. Focus on optimising (there's that word again) your site for its main purpose. As I mentioned a little while ago, our site is designed expressly to get people to sign up for our e-zine. Everything else is secondary.

Your next decision is what to put up on your website. Ultimately, you can put up whatever you and your web designer/blogging platform can dream up. Here, though, is a suggested list of must-have pages:

- Home
- About us
- Services
- Portfolio
- Testimonials
- Contact us

You will probably also want privacy and site usage policy pages. If your site is a custom-built one, you may want to integrate a blog into it and add in other articles, downloads and assorted freebies as it grows.

Do include a mugshot. Remember that although words are your stock-in-trade, people buy from people. It looks odd, to my eye, when a service business built around a single individual has no photos of that individual. It's not that you want to be hired because you're attractive (though it probably doesn't hurt your chances): it's just that it gives your site some personality and helps your visitor connect with the person they'll be hiring.

SEO

I don't propose to lecture you about SEO. The subject changes so fast a printed book is the wrong format for a detailed discussion of what's happening. And also there's a good chance you know more about it than I do. Here, though, are a few thoughts on SEO as it applies to copywriters' sites:

First of all, decide whether search is important to you. I know, I know, this is a bit like asking a racehorse if galloping is important. But think about it for a moment. Who do you want to work for? Is it local firms? Companies in the aerospace industry? Agencies looking for SEO specialists? Next, ask yourself whether these people are using search themselves to find copywriters. If they are, fine, all you need to do is figure out or find out what search terms they're using and weave them into your copy. But maybe the people you want to work for aren't using search. For some reason I keep coming back to the idea of surgeons. If you wanted to find the best heart surgeon in the country, would you load Google and type in "best heart surgeon in England"? You would? Oh, OK, my bad. Skip this section. But I think you would probably start by asking your GP or the cardiology department of your local hospital.

If the whole surgery metaphor isn't working for you, maybe I can just show you how we use the web at Sunfish. First of all, we're not that fussed whether we are found by people Googling "freelance copywriter". We want to work for people who ask their colleagues if they know of a decent subscriptions or direct response copywriter, or someone with experience in publishing or B2B. We want people who read the trade press or books, or attend seminars. Yes they may want to check out our credentials after they have been pointed in our direction by a colleague, but they don't, generally, use search in the first instance.

Direct mail

A couple of years ago we won a big piece of work from a magazine publisher. A dream account in fact – lovely people to work for, exciting (yes, really) brands, long copy and the scope to produce some outstanding creative work too. We got onto the pitch list because the direct marketing manager had met her counterpart at a well known London listings magazine and asked him if he knew of any good subscriptions copywriters. He mentioned me (we had recently worked together on a couple of campaigns), which gave us our foot in the door. So how did I get the listings magazine as a client? I wrote to him. Twice. Here is the first letter:

Dear [name],

I'm writing to introduce my copywriting agency to you.

We are copywriters with a difference. The difference is we specialise in subscriptions copywriting. Everything from acquisitions to welcome packs and renewal series. Online or offline.

Over the last two years we have worked with IPC, Euromoney, the International Herald Tribune, William Reed Business Media, Elsevier, Reed Business Information and Incisive Media.

Whether you want higher renewals, more new subscribers, more RFTs, more additional sales or more gift subscriptions, we've a portfolio stuffed with successful examples and testimonials from your peers in subscriptions marketing. Like this one ...

"I recently contracted Sunfish to write and produce a new renewal series. My brief was understood and interpreted perfectly and we were very pleased with the final outcome."

Tracy Larner, Marketing Manager,
William Reed Business Media

If you're happy with the way things are you won't need us right now. But do please keep our details on file and email me at andy.maslen@sunfish.co.uk if you'd like a no-obligation quote for a piece of copy. Oh, one more thing.

We work closely with a designer on many of the campaigns we write. So if you need design and artwork as well as copy, we can help you there, too.

Yours sincerely,
Andy Maslen F IDM

PS: You can sample our ideas before hiring us by subscribing to our free e-zine, Maslen on Marketing, at www.sunfish.co.uk/subscribe.htm. You get practical tips every month and two free e-books as well.

The second letter was virtually identical, apart from the opening lines. It started like this:

Dear [name],

I wrote to you a while back about our subscriptions copywriting services. You didn't reply then so I'm guessing everything was fine. If things have changed at [company] maybe we could set up a meeting.

The second time I wrote, I got a call. He said my timing was great because things had changed and he now needed some help with a new campaign. I went in for the meeting and got the gig.

So, direct mail can work. But you have to be persistent. You have to keep mailing. And, above all, you have to be lucky with your timing. Unlike tomatoes, toothpaste or tea bags, people tend not to have a year-round need for copywriters. They need us when they need us, not when we need them and decide to write them a letter. That's why I favour the e-zine for our "push" communications. We have the recipients' permission to contact them 12 times a year and that makes it far more likely that one of the issues will coincide with their having a need for our services, whether that's copywriting, coaching, a workshop or even just buying one of my books.

If you are going to do some mailings, then your list is key. Far more important than the copy, in fact. Old direct mail hands know that list quality has a huge impact on responsiveness compared with copy. It doesn't mean you can get away with bad copy, just that in tests, list quality makes more of a difference to your response rate. Here's how to do it. Define your ideal customer first. Let's say, marketing managers working in SMEs within 50 miles of your office. Then contact a reliable list broker, do your own research on the internet or go direct to a list owner. Check what you're entitled to do with the list – is it for a one-time-only mailing or multiple uses for a year? And what's their policy on gone-aways, ie. undeliverable addresses? A while back I did a big competitor analysis project for one of the UK's largest list owners. At that time, most firms in the industry were offering a refund on all undeliverables over 1 per cent of the total list size ordered.

In your letter, think very hard about what you're going to say. Even though we are all professional copywriters, it's surprising how hard it can be to write a good sales letter for our own business. I see plenty that bang on about features, when the reader wants to know about benefits. You could do worse than follow our old friend AIDCA. Just to refresh your memory, that's Attention, Interest, Desire, Conviction, Action.

Maybe direct mail feels a bit old school in the age of Twitter, LinkedIn and the myriad delights of the blogosphere. Well, it is. But it does work.

Seminars/training

Running seminars is a great way of building your reputation as an expert and meeting potential clients.

Running seminars is a great way of building your reputation as an expert and meeting potential clients. You could, say, organise a two-hour seminar on web copywriting at a local hotel, invite a few dozen local businesses and maybe the local press too, with a bit of a networking lunch afterwards. There's a local IT firm in Salisbury, where we're based, which does this all the time. Their seminars are generally an hour long, so people can fit them into their lunch hours.

The beauty of seminars is that although you appear to be training potential clients in how to write copy themselves, the net effect is usually that they realise just how skilled – and difficult – a job it is. And hire you instead.

The question is, do you charge for what, after all, is another sales and marketing channel? And the answer is, yes you do. Not necessarily very much. For a lunchtime seminar I would think £50-£75 would be about right. And here's why you charge. Because if it's free, it doesn't have any value. In my corporate marketing job we used to organise all sorts of events: press launches, products launches, parties. And we discovered that you got a much lower dropout rate if you charged people to attend. That's partly because having paid they want their money's worth. The only time you don't need to charge is if you have one of the following:

a) A stunning venue – the top of the Gherkin for example.

b) A celebrity – come and learn about direct marketing copywriting and meet that bloke off the telly.

c) Free booze (only joking)

Or you could set up copywriting training as a service line in its own right, and charge for it. When I started running training courses for a client of Sunfish, my initial question to their marketing director was, "Aren't I going to be training myself out of a job?" She said, "Not at all. We write so much copy we never commission out that you'd just be doing us a huge favour." Now training and coaching probably accounts for 20 per cent to 30 per cent of our turnover. As that's not really a marketing channel anymore I won't go into detail. But if you have presentation skills (or are prepared to develop them) and you like meeting people face-to-face who could hire you to write copy for them, training is definitely worth thinking about.

Networking

Quite a few of the freelance copywriters I interviewed for this book use networking to meet clients and get referrals. So what are your options? At the local level you have the dedicated networking groups to join. Three of the best-known in the UK are BNI, Ambassadors and 4Networking. The idea is that you go along, have a spot of breakfast, make a short pitch to the other members, listen to theirs and then, hopefully, make contacts that lead to work. There's often a principle of reciprocity involved, where members agree to recommend one another to their networks outside the immediate group they belong to. One aspect I found off-putting when invited to join one of these organisations was the sectoral exclusivity. At first, when we moved to Salisbury I was told that I couldn't join because there was already a freelance copywriter in the group so they weren't accepting any more. You can imagine my response. "Oh fine. Well you can keep your contacts then." (I suspect there was more than a little pique involved in my reaction.) I also couldn't hack the early starts, preferring to be in bed rather than making my way down to the Cathedral cloister restaurant for a 7.30 breakfast meeting.

But there's another aspect to this closed-shop arrangement that gives me pause. It all feels a little bit insular. OK, so you're the only copywriter in the group. Work those contacts for all you're worth. Just as long as you lift your eyes up towards the horizon now and again and realise how many local businesses aren't members. Where are you going to find them?

What about other forms of networking? Here are three I use and a few ideas for making them work for you.

First of all, industry networking. My background is in publishing. When we set up Sunfish it made sense to start with the contacts and the industry I knew, and which knew me. Over the years I have attended publishing conferences and seminars and have found them to be a brilliant source of highly desirable leads. For a start the attendees include lots of marketing managers at publishing companies. And they are all potential clients – no need for those "would you keep me in mind and refer me to your clients?" conversations. The downside is they're not cheap to attend. But in comparison to the potential revenue from projects you pick up, I would say they're worth the investment. You also get to learn a few things from the conference sessions. You can report these in your blog, website or e-zine too, further establishing your reputation. Why not spend a little time finding out whether there are any events for the industries you cover and buy a ticket. Who knows, you might even be able to do a contra-deal with the event organisers: a speech for a place.

Secondly, professional networking. If you're a member of any professional associations or institutes, get along to their networking events. Here you'll meet fellow copywriters and potential clients and they're all happy to talk because that's what these events are for. The Chartered Institute of Marketing and the Institute of Direct Marketing are two that spring to mind straight away.

Last, let's not forget social networking. And no, I don't mean Twitter, Flickr, MySpace and Facebook. I mean social networking such as parties, and dinners and pubs and meeting people while you're pushing your children on the swings. On that last point, when I was a new dad I was indeed pushing my young son on the swings, and I got talking to the mum next to me. "What do you do?" she asked. "I'm a copywriter," I answered. "That's someone who …" "Oh, I know what a copywriter is," she cut in, "I used to be a copywriter at OgilvyOne in Canary Wharf." Cue very interesting conversation.

You might also remember my story from the very beginning of Section Three, about my friend Giles. He was the finance director of a big local company at the time and when I asked for the name of his marketing director he said I should pitch to him. There and then.

This might sound a little cheesy, but you should make a point of having a few business cards on you all the time. You never know whom you'll be standing next to, sipping chilled Sauvignon Blanc at a barbecue. But they could be your next client. Or their sister-in-law could.

A final couple of thoughts on the right way to network. To paraphrase President John F. Kennedy, ask not what this person can do for you, ask what they can do for your network. Yes, by all means pitch your copywriting services to them, but be aware that if they're not looking for a copywriter at the moment, that's going to be a boring conversation. Ask questions and find out what they are looking for. Maybe you know a web designer or a digital printer they could use. They'll be grateful and when they do need a copywriter, you know whom they'll think of first. Second, if someone asks you what you do, have a clear and succinct answer ready to give them. We talked about your elevator pitch in Section Three. Remember that not everyone knows what a copywriter does (it's surprising how many think it's something to do with copyright). Focus on explaining what you can do for them and their business. That's what they'll find interesting and get them asking you questions. Then you can explain you write SEO copy, mailshots, corporate brochures or press releases.

Public speaking

Let's try a simple test. Imagine you're in a small room with two doors. One labelled "Public Speaking" and the other labelled "Wisdom Teeth Extraction". Coming towards you across the floor is a great big hairy spider. Which door do you make for? If you're like most people, you will probably find yourself in the dentist's chair, not on the speaker's rostrum. Which is a problem. Because public speaking is a really great way to build your reputation and win new clients. Not just any clients either, the kind who want to hire experts. And you know the great thing about being an expert, don't you? They get paid more.

I think it's worth conquering any fear you may have of public speaking because, unlike social media, the entire focus of the audience is on you. Yes, yes, I know that's what gives you the willies. Me too. But people come up to you afterwards and say things like, "That was really interesting, here's a million pounds to rewrite our corporate marketing campaign." Well, something like that anyway. And you get to post your speech as an article on your website and blog. And the event organisers will probably ask you for a podcast and stick it on their site.

Try to conquer any fears you have about public speaking: it's worth persevering with because public speaking also encompasses training courses and seminars and these are very lucrative territory for a copywriter.

Social media

I'm veering dangerously close to membership of the old farts club, which doesn't preclude my discussing social media; but it's not my main marketing channel and there are plenty of other sources of information about how to make it (them?) work for you. Here are my thoughts.

Embrace social media. This is a financially cheap option for marketing your business. There are opportunity costs, however, since every five minutes you spend on Twitter is five minutes you can't spend telephoning potential clients and selling. Still and all, if you like it and it feels right to you, register, create accounts and log in to every social networking site you can find.

Or don't. A friend of mine has a client who told her he knew he ought to be on Facebook. "Don't do it because you 'ought' to," she counselled. "Do it because you want to." If you're not a natural social media user and every tweet, poke and fiddle (I made that one up) feels like a chore, it will sound like it's a chore and won't get you anywhere.

And don't kid yourself that tweeting is the same as selling. You might feel busy, but I don't think you're going to get rich via Twitter. It's best to view social media as an adjunct to your main direct channels of communication with your market. You simply can't create the same impact in an individual client's mind as you can with a well written and targeted email, letter, meeting or phone call. Feel free to disagree, violently even, and get in touch with your evidence that I'm spouting nonsense.

Embrace social media. This is a financially cheap option for marketing your business.

Advertising

Press advertising? I'd forget it. Unless you get an ad in exchange for an article in a contra-deal with a magazine publisher, they're not worth it. You have to advertise repeatedly over a long period to really generate any return on investment for a service-based business such as copywriting. It's ironic given how many of us write ads for a living. It can work if you have a product to sell, like a book or a training course, but I would still crunch the numbers until they're reduced to dust before you invest.

Pay-per-click, on the other hand? Yes, why not. Or maybe not. You know what they say about horses being led to water. It's fairly easy to write and design an AdWords campaign and have punters flocking to your site, lured, perhaps, by the promise of a free download, an e-zine or some other enticing goody. But conversions are where it's at and you can still end up paying a hefty bill to Google at the end of each month without very much to show for it. My experience of AdWords is that the conversion rate wasn't justifying the cost (we want people to sign up for our e-zine). Of course that could say more about the design of our landing page than the efficacy of AdWords as a route to market for copywriters. The advice here is simple: test, measure and evaluate. And don't focus on click-throughs. That way penury lies.

Blog

Blogging is a bit like social media. You can spend an awful lot of time doing it for not very much financial return.

Blogging is a bit like social media. You can spend an awful lot of time doing it for not very much return. Financial return, I mean. And what could you be doing instead? As a brand-building tool it can work, although you have to be careful that you're building your brand with the right people. It doesn't matter how many other freelance copywriters read your blog (and this has to be one of the biggest audiences), the question is, how many potential or actual clients are reading it? I get a sense that the copywriting blogosphere is, like many other professional spaces, fairly inward-looking. We all read each other's blogs, post comments and tweet about interesting posts. What I haven't seen much evidence of, for example, is marketing managers at large corporations tweeting about blog posts they've read. I suspect they are all too busy.

If your blog, which you can set up in minutes, is read by lots of clients (actual or potential) that's brilliant, frankly. Just so long as you convert those readers into customers.

SECTION 7
SELLING YOURSELF AND YOUR BUSINESS, AND WHY IT'S DIFFERENT TO MARKETING

It's not about knowing how to spell, it's about knowing how to sell.

Let's assume that one or more of your chosen marketing channels is paying off. Your inbox is bulging with leads. The next question is, what are you going to do about them? Or, to put it another way, can you close? Because it's all very well having enquiries, but if you can't convert enquirers into customers, you might as well go home. Oh, I forgot, you are at home. Well, you might as well go to the gym then. I don't think there are many freelance copywriters who would say they actively enjoy selling, but it's just about the most important skill you can possess if you want to make a go of it. And yes, I am including writing in that list. If you can sell well and write poorly you will still make a better living than someone else who can write brilliantly but can't sell. As my interviewee Claire McCarthy says, "It's not about knowing how to spell, it's about knowing how to sell". I can't improve on that.

But what does it actually mean, to be good at selling? Well, you could start by thinking about your own business the way you do about your clients'. Here are a few questions to get you started:

Exercise 5 – Learning to sell yourself

1. What are the benefits of hiring you to write copy?

Given that this is a fairly standard exercise and every copywriter will come up with the same list, the next question is more pertinent. But answer this one anyway.

_____

_____

_____

_____

_____

_____

_____

_____

2. What are the benefits of hiring you rather than anyone else to write copy?

Now we're getting somewhere. What is it about you and your approach, credentials or background that mean your clients should trust you to write their copy rather than that other copywriter in your town. This is really important because it feeds into any conversations you have about your prices.

_____

_____

_____

_____

_____

_____

_____

_____

3. What objections might someone have to hiring you?

This might make you feel a bit vulnerable, especially because for this question to work you have to be honest, brutally so, about your own shortcomings as perceived by clients. But you must be honest. Are you expensive (whatever you understand that to mean)? Inexperienced? Based in Timbaktu? Write it down.

_____

_____

_____

_____

_____

_____

_____

_____

4. How do you overcome those objections?

OK, this is your chance to lose those feelings of vulnerability and turn them into feelings of confidence. "Based in Timbaktu? True, but I find email and Skype mean I can handle projects for clients all over the world. In fact one of my clients is based in New Zealand and we've never met."

_____

_____

_____

_____

_____

_____

_____

_____

5. If someone queries your fees what are you going to say to them?

Remember, your first answer is never, "OH, OK then, what can you afford?" or anything like that.

_____

_____

_____

_____

_____

_____

_____

_____

Sales meetings: what clients want to hear (and what they don't)

In my experience, once you've managed to get that precious meeting with a potential client, there is a very simple and effective way to screw it up. Here's what you do. You start talking. About yourself. And you don't stop. I know this because I used to do it. Until I noticed the dead-eyed expression on the faces of my prospects. Then I learned to do something different. I asked questions. If you've read my first book, *Write to Sell,* you may remember the time I went to Frankfurt to meet some executives from Panasonic. No sooner had we sat down than I launched into a 45-minute history of my company and every single one of its products. None of which the Panasonic guys were interested in. Finally, when I paused for breath, they said they wanted to know about the European market for domestic air conditioning units. Aha!

So, in response to the heading at the top of this section, clients don't want to hear about you. What they do want to hear about is ... you guessed it ... themselves. Here's a simple opening that unlocks the potential for paid copywriting work.

"Thanks for agreeing to see me. So tell me about your current marketing goals. What are you trying to achieve?"

Then shut up. Your prospect will cheerfully spend the next ten or fifteen minutes telling you all about their business and what they're trying to do with it. Here's another piece of advice. Take notes. Lots of notes. Look up into their eyes from time to time and nod to show you are listening, but take notes. Two reasons why. First, you need the notes when it comes to responding in this meeting and also later on when you come back with your proposal or quotation. Second, it shows you are interested in what they're saying. I know you are interested, but note-taking shows them you are.

If your prospect asks you a question, about your experience, or specialism, then get going with your pitch. But remember

Take notes. Lots of notes. Look up into their eyes from time to time and nod to show you are listening, but take notes.

this. They would still rather be doing the talking, so keep your answer brief and to the point. Nobody cares how you got into copywriting, or where you work or whether you've always loved writing. As soon as you can, steer the conversation back to your prospect and their needs. The more you understand about their needs the more you can offer the right solution, whether that's copywriting, name creation, some consulting or maybe a bit of copywriting training.

As the meeting draws to a close, remember your call to action. If you have discussed fees in the meeting, now is the time to close them. "So, when do you want me to start?" could work. So could, "Do you want to go ahead then?" It doesn't really matter what you say as long as you put them on the spot and ask for the order. Many freelance copywriters, I imagine, shy away from this crunch-time question, fearing that they will get a "No". Well, you might. You might also get a "Yes" though. And if you do get the wrong answer you now have the chance to ask why and see if you can turn them around. Refer back to your answers to Exercise 5 on objection handling. If you ask them why they don't want to go ahead they will give you their reason. Maybe it's based on a misreading of something you've said. Maybe they have an unanswered question you can put them straight on here and now. If you don't ask, you'll never know.

If you haven't discussed fees, and the next step is for you to come back to them with a quotation, make sure you know exactly what they're expecting, and when. Leave the meeting with an agreement that you are going to do X by Y, and they are going to respond by Z. And ask when it would be convenient for you to call them back to see how they feel about your proposal.

To cold call or not to cold call?

After public speaking, I reckon calling strangers on the phone ranks right up there for most freelancers as an activity they'd walk over broken glass to avoid. That's broken glass someone's set on fire first. And stuck in cement so the pointy bits face upwards. Which is a shame because it's really effective for winning business. So why the reluctance? Mining my own feelings for the answers, here are a few possibilities:

- They might reject me.
- I might not get through.
- Suppose they get cross because I've interrupted their day.
- I'll feel embarrassed.
- They might be a lot more senior than me.

And here are a few possible retorts to those fears:

- They might not. They might hire you.
- Leave a message or tell the person you speak to you'll try later.
- Politely get off the phone as quickly as you can.
- Practise your opening line and remember you can help them out of a tight spot.
- So? They still use the lavatory like everybody else. Imagine them there.

When I was just starting out as a freelance copywriter, I called a potential client at a business information publisher. I made my pitch and he said:

> "Fine. Here's what I suggest. We have an integrated marketing campaign on at the moment for a new banking directory. Come in and spend a couple of days selling it on the phone. If you can shift a few copies I'll hire you to write some copy for the direct mail campaign."

gulp
"Yes, that sounds great," I said. "Shall we say tomorrow at 9.00 am?"

I did go in and I did sit with a phone and a list of senior banking contacts and I did sell a couple of dozen copies and I did get hired to write the copy. Phew. By the way, he paid me £100 a day for my sales calls. A lot less than the figure I had calculated should be my day rate.

Here are a few thoughts on how to take the sting out of cold calling. And for this section I am assuming we're talking about calling clients direct. Not having worked for agencies I can't be sure about this, but I imagine there's no real problem with a freelance copywriter calling the creative director of an agency. They expect it and probably welcome it. So...

Maybe you can turn cold calling into warm calling by sending an email (or better still, a letter) first. Then when you call your prospect you can open like this:

"Hello, Mr Jones? [Or Sam?, if you feel that will work better] It's Andy Maslen here from Sunfish: I sent you a letter about our copywriting services."
[they reply]
If they say yes they remember it, you say: "What did you think?"

This is a pretty open-ended question, which is good because now they have to tell you something. If you ask them whether it was of interest, they can simply shut you down by saying no. End of call.

If they say no, they don't remember it, you have the chance to make a brief pitch. And I mean brief. A couple of sentences. Maybe use your elevator pitch or a variant of it. As soon as you can you ask them a question.

"I'm just calling to enquire whether you have any campaigns on the go that I could help you with."

Here you are going to get a yes/no answer. If it's a no here's what you say:

"OK, I understand. Would it be OK if I gave you a courtesy call in a few months to see if anything has changed?"

The word "courtesy" is key, as it now would seem churlish to turn down your request. You thank them, wish them a good day and get off the line. Make a note in your diary to call them in three months and go on to your next call.

If you don't feel the need to warm them up first (and bear in mind the person who's really being warmed up is you) you can try the approach we discussed in Section 3. You know, where you call the switchboard of the companies you want to work for and ask for the name of the marketing director.

Then you pick ten of your prospects. You make a little pile of ten paperclips on the right-hand side of your desk (or the left, I'm not going to get all Terminator over this), and for each call you make, you move one of your paperclips over to the other side of your desk. When all ten have moved you get to have a chocolate biscuit. Or a stiff drink.

Then you dial the first number. Here's what you say:

Receptionist: Thank you for calling Watkins Widgets of Wolverhampton, Jane speaking, how may I direct your call today?

You: Hello, Martin Smith here, of Wordsmith; could you put me through to Byron Brown please?

If he's out you ask when he'll next be in the office and say you'll call back, remembering to thank the receptionist.

If the receptionist asks "Will he know what it's about?" you resist the temptation to say "Not unless he's psychic, no". Instead you say:

You: It's about helping him increase sales this year.

I defy any receptionist not to put that call through.

Byron Brown:	Byron Brown.
You:	Mr Brown – it's Martin Smith here. I run a small copywriting agency here in Wolverhampton and I hope I can help you increase your sales this year.
BB:	Oh really, how are you going to do that then?
You:	Well, I write marketing and sales copy for growing businesses that brings in more leads and orders. In fact what I'd reallylike to do is come and see you so I can find out a bit more about your marketing goals for this year.

Do you get the picture? I'm going to stop the dialogue here, partly because as I'm making this up it gets a bit pointless. I could have Byron offering you the job of chief copywriter in perpetuity if I felt like it. And partly because I think you're smart enough to figure out how to get from here to the meeting.

Building relationships

Early on in my career as a freelancer, I imagined how grand it would sound to tell people my clients included *The Economist,* The London Stock Exchange, and Hamleys. Then I learned an important lesson. Your clients aren't companies, they're people. Yes, at the time they hire you they happen to work at this big blue chip agency or corporate client, but they hired you, not WCRS, Saatchis or Tesco. This is good news. Because building relationships with people is a) easier than doing it with brands, b) more rewarding on a personal level and c) likely to stand you in good stead when the inevitable happens. What is the inevitable? They leave their job.

This can either be a disaster or a boon to your business. It's a disaster if you haven't invested sufficient time in developing a strong personal relationship with your client. Your client leaves, probably without letting you know, because why would they? You call next month to be told "Oh, Dawn doesn't work here anymore." This leaves you looking foolish (how come you didn't know that?) and also without a contact at your former client company. You also don't know where Dawn has gone so you have to start rebuilding your network.

It's a boon, on the other hand, if you have a warm relationship with Dawn. She'll probably tell you before she's handed in her notice that she's thinking of making a move, and she'll certainly let you know when she's going, and where. You may even get invited to her leaving drinks (I have been on occasion). Play your cards right and Dawn will even introduce you to her successor, giving you a fighting chance of hanging on to the gig. This doesn't always play well, because incoming marketing managers or creative directors frequently have their own favourite freelancers (just as outgoing ones do) and will be more likely to want to work with them than you. But you never know.

Relationship-based marketing, if we can call it that, is great because you don't have to keep pitching. Your client (that's a person, remember) just calls you and commissions more copy. They move, settle in and, yes, you guessed it, call you and ask to you to write more copy. In economic terms, this type of work is vastly more profitable than the more transactional style of project where you have to win every job from scratch.

Favours

Although earlier in this book I counselled against giving away your knowledge and services, there are times when it can pay off. One of them is when you have a good client and you are in a position to do them a favour. Maybe they need you to look over a short piece of copy and simply don't have any budget. Twenty minutes of your time and it's done. You've made your client's little headache go away and they will remember the favour. Or they ask you if you know anything about the latest trends in, oh, I don't know, SEO copywriting or social media. Give them a quick rundown on what's out there, point them at a couple of blogs or websites and, again, it's a favour they should remember. Lest this all sounds a little bit calculating, I should say that the starting point is that you like each other. It's natural to want to do favours for friends, and over the years, I have met lots of people who started off as clients pure and simple, but whom I now regard as friends.

Where's the brief? Get it in writing...or take the consequences

One of the most common subjects for disagreements between freelancer and client is whether the former has delivered copy that the latter was expecting. They may not like it, which is a tricky one, because with every fibre of your being you may want to shout, "You're not meant to like it, you're meant to profit from it!" But let's be honest, if they don't like it (an emotional reaction) they probably won't pay you for it, so you might as well produce something they do like. Or they may feel that you haven't written copy that meets the brief (a rational reaction). The next question is, where's the brief?

It pays to get a written brief. However strong your relationship with your client, nothing beats a written brief for ending arguments before they've begun. Better than ending arguments, the brief is there to ensure you both agree on what you're writing before you start. And here's another point to consider. When you're discussing the project with your client, ask them who else will be involved in approving your copy. Suggest, politely, that these people should also sign off the brief. That way, when you deliver your first draft, everyone says, "Oh yes, that's what we discussed in our conference call. Look, they've included all the sections we discussed and written it in a tone of voice half-way between a revivalist preacher and a gangsta rapper." Or words to that effect.

It pays to get a written brief. However strong your relationship with your client, nothing beats a written brief for ending arguments before they've begun.

Testimonials...uncovering your best sales people

You know the C in AIDCA? It stands for Conviction. One of the best ways to convince someone you're a good bet is to offer them a testimonial. Better yet, lots of testimonials. From your very first job, make it your mission to collect them. The best kind, because they are usually couched in emphatic, emotional and very believable language, are the unsolicited emails (or, increasingly rarely these days, letters) from delighted clients. When you receive one of these here's what I advise you to do. Ping back an email immediately saying something like this:

> *Dear Isabel,*
>
> *Thank you so much for you kind words about the ad copy I wrote for you. I really hope it helps build your brand/sell some [product].*
> *Would you mind if I quoted you on the testimonials page of my website?*
>
> *Best wishes,*
> *Elaine*

Clients are usually pleased that you're pleased (it all gets a bit circular here) and will happily consent.

If you don't get any unsolicited testimonials, don't worry. Solicit some instead. Maybe with an email like this one:

> *Dear Isabel,*
>
> *I am just putting together a marketing campaign for [your company]. Would you mind writing me a testimonial about the [project] I wrote for you last month? I know*

*you're busy so if you'd prefer me to draft something for
you to edit/amend, just let me know.*

*Best regards,
Elaine*

Clients, again, are usually happy to help and as they are usually busy, will often ask you to write something for them. If they do, avoid the temptation to get too gushy. Or to write something "professional" sounding. Be as natural as you can manage and aim for the tone of voice and style your client would use.

Making yourself look and sound good

One final thought on selling and salesmanship. You need to dress the part. If you're phoning prospects from your home office, I suggest you get dressed up. Not just your work clothes – jeans or trackie bottoms or whatever – I mean something smart. Something sharp. You'll sit straighter. In fact you won't sit straighter because I also recommend that you make these incredibly important calls standing up. You feel more confident and your voice production is better because your lungs aren't squashed between your ribs and your diaphragm.

And when you go for that meeting, get suited and booted (this goes for men and women). Yes, you are in a "creative" job (and we'll skip the rant about creativity for now) but you are also in business, as is your prospect. I tend to go for a suit and tie. Even if you end up dressed more smartly than your client, it never hurts to be one tick higher on the sartorial sharpness scale than them and, again, it shows respect. If that's too much, then at the very least, smart trousers/skirt and jacket. Choose bright accessories (cufflinks, bag etc) if you want to look creative. But just remember this: if they hire you it's because they think you can help them make a lot of extra money – and that's serious business.

I always feel more confident if I have cool stuff to take into meetings with me. A nice leather notebook. A gorgeous Waterman fountain pen. A battered, but very high-end leather briefcase. Sometimes they're talking points in their own right, but in any case they make me feel like I can win any job.

Finally, your voice. I don't suggest you take elocution lessons. But if you feel nerves sometimes get the better of you and you know it makes you speak quietly or stutter a little, just practise your opening lines in front of the mirror. Getting that crucial handshake-and-pleasantries stage out of the way without fluffing it puts you and your prospect at ease. You just need to sound like yourself and remember that even if you are facing the CEO of a Fortune 500 company, they are still just a human being.

SECTION 8
DESIGN AND WHAT TO DO ABOUT IT

You should write copy with a view to its eventual look and feel.

Copy and design are intertwined to such an extent that although you can write copy for clients without ever considering design, I think you'd be a fool to do so. Why a fool? Because there are lots of benefits to you that flow from a grasp of the basics. Let's run through them.

Why you need to know about design

First of all, if you have a basic grasp of design terminology – for print, online or both – you can have more productive meetings and discussions with your clients. When they start asking about how this line would work as a marquee rather than a headline, or whether you think it would be OK as a banner as a well as a skyscraper, well, you need to have a sensible answer don't you?

There are plenty of places where you can pick up a good design vocabulary so I don't propose to lecture you here about the difference between serif and sans serif typefaces; leading, layout and look-and-feel; packshots and palettes; breadcrumb trails, wireframes and the rest. Make it your business to learn about the most relevant aspects of design for the types of projects you work on. If you never write for print, then foil-blocking, trim marks and concertina folds will be an irrelevance. If you only write corporate brochures then animated GIFs, Flash intros and anchor text will, equally, be things you can ignore. But what happens when your favourite client asks whether you have any bright ideas for a new brochure they're putting together that people can download from their site? Or when your corporate communications manager chum suggests you'd be just right for their new microsite and what do you think about embedding text in images? The more you know about design, the more you will look like an attractive bet, since you can offer advice as well as copy. Which makes you sound like an expert. And what's our mantra about experts? All together now:

"Experts can charge more for their services."

Here's another huge reason to get your design knowledge polished up. The likelihood of your being rehired depends to a large extent on the success or failure of the campaign you write copy for. So anything you can do to increase the chances of a positive outcome is to the good. Making sure the design enhances the copy and doesn't detract from it has to be a good thing. And if you're going to do that, you're going to have to have an intelligent discussion with a designer/art director. Which will be difficult if you don't speak their language.

If you're writing copy for any kind of direct response campaign, online or offline, then the response mechanism is key. So whether you're writing sales letters with integral coupons, brochures with order forms, e-commerce pages or landing pages, knowing how forms work is a real advantage. Here, my biggest tip is to ensure that the form is easy to fill in. If I had a pound for every form I've seen that had some problem with its fill-in-ability, oh, you know the rest.

Finally, and this is part of the job to do with your craftsmanship or womanship, you should write copy with a view to its eventual look and feel. It won't ever appear simply as plain text so you need to specify, or at least suggest, how headings, captions and other devices should work. I call them stage directions and always treat them the same way in my drafts: [I put my suggestions inside square brackets].

Do you need a partner?

I've already mentioned my friend and design partner Ross Speirs. Way back before I was doing the freelance thing, we were having lunch one day and he said, "You know, I wonder whether we should try working on a project together. I haven't said anything sooner because I didn't want to ruin our friendship if anything

Experts can charge more for their services.

went wrong." I said, "That's just what I was thinking." So, once we'd got our mutual friendship anxiety out of the way, we did start working together. I would write the copy for our mailshots and brochures and I hired Ross to do the design. It was a natural evolution that once I set up Sunfish, we would carry on the partnership. Very quickly, I got asked by a client to produce a mailshot for a computer magazine. She didn't want just copy, she wanted an agency that could do everything, right up to print-ready artwork. Here's a tip for early days selling. When a client asks you, "Do you do this?", as long as you think you can do it, you say "Yes". And say it straight away. Figure out the finer points on how later. (I'm assuming the task in question is at least tangentially related to copywriting, which you do well. Flying a stunt plane at the CEO's birthday party would be a simple "no". Or would it? I leave it to you.)

So I said "yes", gave Ross a call and we delivered the mailshot as requested. Two interesting consequences of that initial project. One, Ross and I have worked on hundreds of projects since even, though we are neither of us employees of each other's companies or contracted in any way to each other. Two, we are still creating mailshots for that publisher 12 years and several direct marketing managers later.

That's rather a long answer. The shorter answer is, you don't need a partner, but it's a very useful route to extra income. Here's why. If you can offer design as part of the package, you will probably pick up jobs that you would miss if you could only write copy. I have definitely won projects because the client wanted a complete creative package. You can also strike a mutually profitable agreement with your designer friend where they give you a trade discount in return for bringing in extra work. The client pays the same – this is important, as selling marked-up design fees puts you at a disadvantage in the marketplace – and benefits from having a single point of contact for the complete project: you. Here's the caveat...

Make sure you trust them. I once worked with a different designer when Ross was snowed under with work. He was a lot cheaper than Ross so for a few projects my income looked much juicier. But then he screwed up royally on a job, sending only half the artwork to my very best client on an extremely urgent job. I found out because she called me on my mobile. I was in the middle of town at the time and ran, literally, all the way back to my office to start making calls and sorting things out. I never used that guy again, and now, if Ross is busy, or out of the country, I tell clients they can wait for him to get back or choose someone else themselves, but he's the only designer I use through Sunfish.

Another reason to find a design partner is that just as you bring them work, they should be able to bring you work. Designers often get approached by clients looking for a new website or brochure only to find the copy supplied is not up to the job. It's usually been written by the MD, the IT manager (if it's a website) or a brand new marketing assistant, none of whom has the training for the job and none of whom should therefore be blamed for doing the best they can with limited tools. When this happens you want your designer buddy to be putting your name forward as a safe pair of hands for the job. How you handle the billing is up to you. I think it's only fair that if someone's sales and marketing efforts bring you a job, you show your appreciation financially. You could offer them a trade discount and effectively bill through them. Or you could bill the client direct and let your design partner bill you for a finder's fee. It doesn't matter, it's your call and whatever you do that you both agree on is obviously fine. One last thing: you might want to agree that the person sub-contracting gets paid when the main contractor gets paid. Saves trouble later on.

A final thought on design, which I mention only because I saw, some time ago, an e-zine article asserting that there was an easy way to add £300 to any copywriting job you win. The "easy way" was to do the design yourself as well. This leads, I think, to problems. Unless you are supremely talented, and have invested in the hardware, software, image library subscriptions and fonts you're going to need, avoid claiming you can handle design. You spend time convincing clients copywriting is a skilled profession so doesn't blow it by simultaneously suggesting that design can be done by anyone with a copy of Photoshop, InDesign or Dreamweaver. Mastering one trade is hard enough, let alone two, and believe me, the overheads are a lot lower in ours.

SECTION 9
INTERVIEWS WITH FREELANCE COPYWRITERS

Be ready to sell – work won't always land in your in-box. You need to be ready to be your company's salesman, admin team, accounts department and more.

OK, you've probably had enough of my opinions by now. So here's your chance to hear from 16 very different freelance copywriters. I interviewed these wonderful men and women, mostly by email and a couple by phone, to get their take on the job – from highs and lows to pricing strategy and advice for those just starting out. Before we get to their individual interviews though, I thought you might find it interesting to read a summary of their answers.

Analysis of our interview sample

How did I pick my interviewees? It was anything but scientific, and definitely not random. I asked copywriters I could see following me on Twitter, those who subscribe to my monthly e-zine, a couple of very good friends, and a few I found by Googling "freelance copywriter".

Location
They are based in Norwich, Milton Keynes/Malta, Brighton, Richmond-upon-Thames, Ipswich (2), Hitchin, London (4), Cape Town, Bristol, Tintern, Manchester and Consett.

Gender
There are seven men and nine women.

Experience
Together they have 107.5 years' experience (so do please learn from their wisdom). The average is about 6.5 years; the highest is 17, the lowest 2.5.

Previous job
Before starting work as freelance copywriters, four were working as ad agency copywriters – the most common job among our

sample. After that, their previous roles included marketing manager for a small company; editor at a small publisher; manager at a large corporate; web design agency content writer; copywriter for a large corporate; comms and PR specialist for a large corporate; marketing manager for a small publisher (x2); IT sales; publications/communications officer for a charity; charity assistant; and insurance underwriter.

Reasons for moving into freelancing

Their reasons for making the move into freelance copywriting were redundancy (five people); some sort of epiphany or realisation that copywriting was what they really wanted to do; post-baby career change; a golden opportunity presenting itself; and lifestyle/location changes.

Business/marketing plan

Ten of our sample had no business or marketing plan at all. Six had some kind of plan, but not much. None had anything a bank or a strategy consultant would be happy with. Go figure.

Office and business style

When it comes to office space, 14 work at home and two sublet space from another company. Five are limited companies; 11 are sole traders.

To specialise or not to specialise

Five call themselves specialists, ten say they are generalists and one is both.

Direct or agency

Four work mainly for direct clients, 12 work for a mixture of clients and agencies and none say they work mainly for agencies.

Highs/lows

When we look at their highs/lows of freelance copywriting, the picture looks pretty good, I'd say. Here's the list of reasons they give for enjoying freelancing:

- Variety
- Work/life balance
- Flexibility
- Freedom
- Independence
- Job satisfaction
- Working conditions
- Thinking time
- Money

On the debit side, they cite the following as the worst bits:

- Peaks and troughs of work
- Stress/uncertainty
- Criticism
- Not switching off
- Low status
- Social isolation
- Being a jack-of-all-trades/admin
- Lack of IT support
- Money worries

Sales and marketing channels

In terms of sales and marketing channels, these guys use everything, from Twitter and social networking sites to real networking, sales calls, and direct mail. What works best for our copywriters? Ranked in order of popularity with my interviewees:

1st	Networking (virtual and face-to-face)
2nd	Word-of-mouth/recommendations
3rd	Website
4th	Blogging/agency relationships
5th	Direct mail/emailing clients

Billing

When it comes to billing (and these numbers total more than 16 because some people bill in more than one way), by the project gets nine votes, by the hour gets seven, by the day gets six, and by the word gets three.

Advice for freelancers

Their excellent advice on making a go of freelancing is too varied and individual to be capable of analysis (a good thing), so read on…

The interviews

*The following interviews are **verbatim and unedited**.*

Tom Albrighton

www.abccopywriting.com

Your background

How long have you been working as a freelance copywriter?
Since 2005.

What were you doing before that?
I worked in a small publishing house/design studio. Before that I'd worked for several years at a medium-sized book publisher. At both companies, my job title was 'editor' or 'senior editor' – although my roles involved writing, it wasn't my core responsibility.

What was the event or motivation that led to your decision to move into freelancing?
My employer took a new direction, abandoning publishing, and my post was made redundant. With no obvious new position to go to, I decided to try freelancing in a spirit of 'give it a try and see where it leads'. At that stage, I still thought in terms of freelance equivalents for my 'job description' responsibilities – the idea of positioning myself as a more marketing-focused copywriter came later.

What sort of business or marketing plan did you have when you started out?
I didn't. I really was just giving it a go. But I had some web skills so I could create my own website. For new business, I had a couple of contacts and I applied for some freelance opportunities I saw advertised. I didn't get any work from my former employer. And

it grew from there, principally through word of mouth. Later on, I started to be much more disciplined about doing my own marketing, particularly search marketing, but it's still fairly haphazard because paid work always comes first if you've got dependants.

Where is your office (work at home/sublet space, etc)?
I work at home. I rented a small office for a while, before we moved house, but much prefer home working. My daughter prefers it too, since she can disturb me on an ad hoc basis rather than at specific times.

Are you a sole trader, partnership or limited company?
Limited company. Becoming a company was a very important step in the development of my business. Incorporation puts distance between your own needs and those of the business, and between your funds and the business's, and is worthwhile for that reason alone.

Working as a freelance copywriter

Do you specialise in any industry or form of copywriting, or are you a generalist? Whichever way you work, what do you see as the advantages of that?
I do anything, but my strongest areas are B2B marketing, academic editing and online/SEO. I'm less experienced in B2C, and often decline direct response jobs because I've done so few of them and can't offer enough expertise. However, some smaller clients use me even for my weaker areas, because I've become their 'go-to guy'.

It's certainly worthwhile having some specialisations. It gives focus, and it's a good way to bridge the gap from salary-job competencies to freelance services. You don't have to decline anything just because it falls outside your nominal skillset.

I think most people regard a 'jack of all trades' as a lower-level supplier rather than an established expert – in any area of life. But, as in other areas, people still prosper at those levels and perhaps just feel comfortable as generalists.

Do you work for agencies or direct for clients or a mixture?
A mixture.

What do see as the best thing about working as a freelance copywriter?
Variety. In one day, I might work on three or four completely different topic areas, for clients in three or four different countries. Even though the tasks themselves may not be that demanding or novel for me, the client variety adds more than enough interest.

And the worst?
Lowliness. Although you don't have one single boss as a freelance, you do have lots of 'mini-bosses' in the form of your clients. Some will be nice because of their personal character, but you have to be prepared to have emails unanswered, work questioned and feelings bruised. Unlike an employee, you have no status or authority to call on; it's rarely in anyone's interest to back you up. That can be depressing, particularly as you get older. I like to think I could have been a manager by now (age 38) if I'd stayed in salaried positions, but as a freelancer I'm stuck to the bottom of the food chain. Often, I'm briefed and managed by people with far less experience than me.

Sales and marketing
What sales/marketing channels do you use?
Pay-per-click advertising, article marketing, online PR, online networking (e.g. LinkedIn), optimisation for natural search and social media (e.g. Twitter). Very occasionally, I'll do some offline advertising (e.g. paid directory listing) if the cost is low enough to warrant taking a punt, but I'd never bank on getting results through offline channels.

Which works best for you?

Natural search, which is the result of a combination of on-page optimisation and link-building, on an ongoing basis. However, word of mouth delivers far better leads than the internet ever can – it's just a shame that it can take so long to build a really valuable personal network.

How do you charge for your services? By the hour/day/project/ other?

My own charging basis is by the day, with many part-days (halves or thirds) for smaller projects. I prefer not to charge by the hour, and usually refuse to charge by the word. There's a trend towards buying online content by the word these days, but that type of service has little in common with a professional copywriter's collaborative, service-based approach.

If the client proposes (or counter-offers) a flat fee for a project, I'm often happy to accept it. I always want to make it work for both parties, and it's useful to have a concrete insight into what they regard as reasonable.

Advice

What are the most important skills you need to be a successful freelance copywriter?

Practical writing skill is important – that is, the ability to write text to order, and on time, that achieves its desired purpose (as opposed to 'pure' creative writing).

The ability to manage a small business, keep on top of admin and motivate yourself to get the work done is vital.

On the personal level, you need self-belief, self-responsibility and (sometimes) a thick skin.

If you were starting out again, what would you do differently (if anything)?

I spent too long thinking of my freelance work in terms of the salaried positions I'd held. For example, the fact I'd worked as an editor led me to downplay my commercial writing capability, when in fact my business experience had given me enough knowledge to write commercially. So I'd advise new freelances to 'think outside the box' in terms of configuring their work and life experiences into a set of writing specialisations. You probably know more than you think, so don't limit yourself.

What advice would you to give to someone considering starting out as a freelance copywriter?
- Write a lot, for practice – a blog is a good way to do this.
- Think about how your existing skills and experience could be turned into writing specialisations. Everyone knows about something.
- Always look for ways to add value over and above the actual words you deliver to the client. Again, an existing professional background could be the starting point for this – for example, an accountant might do well writing authoritative FAQs, blog posts and white papers for financial firms, and advising them how to position their services.
- Evaluate your skills realistically, and believe in them firmly.
- Stay attuned to opportunity – it often comes in an unexpected form, or from an unexpected source.
- Critique writing in your areas of expertise – for example, think how an article or editorial in your favourite magazine could be improved.
- Remember that ideas about writing quality, writing style and appropriate fees are largely subjective, and there is no right or wrong answer. Going along with a client's view doesn't mean you agree with it.
- Think very carefully about what you will actually gain by taking a very low-paid job, offering big discounts or working for free. Experience is important, but so are perceptions of value.

Matt Ambrose

http://copywriterscrucible.com

Your background

How long have you been working as a freelance copywriter?
4 years.

What were you doing before that?
Climbing the corporate ladder at Argos.

What was the event or motivation that led to your decision to move into freelancing?
I was sat in an interview for a buying role when I started questioning what I was doing there and why I'd studied English at university in the first place. When I got home I spent all evening on the internet investigating my options. After learning about copywriting I spent the next few months gaining rudimentary skills, creating a portfolio and building a website. Once I'd secured my first client I made the jump into freelancing full-time. Thought it was a risk worth taking (and it was).

What sort of business or marketing plan did you have when you started out?
I had no prior experience (other than an English degree), but did have some savings. So I decided to give myself six months to find out whether I could sustain a full-time living or at least build enough of a portfolio to get local marketing agencies interested. Thankfully, I managed to catch a few lucky breaks and keep going.

Where is your office (work at home/sublet space, etc)?
Currently an apartment in Malta overlooking Balluta Bay.

163

Are you a sole trader, partnership or limited company?
Sole trader.

Working as a freelance copywriter

Do you specialise in any industry or form of copywriting, or are you a generalist? Whichever way you work, what do you see as the advantages of that?
Currently a generalist, but plan on specialising in the future. Being a generalist helps me build up my knowledge on a wide range of topics before deciding what to specialise in. Current areas of expertise include pharmaceuticals (i.e. pharmacies), electronics manufacturing, eco furniture and industrial PCs.

Do you work for agencies or direct for clients or a mixture?
Both. I receive projects from smaller companies through my website and do a lot of work for a marketing agency, which gives me access to larger clients.

What do see as the best thing about working as a freelance copywriter?
Work/life balance – being able to play golf or spend a couple of hours at the beach knowing I can make up for it in the evening. Saving time from not having to commute. Being able to make my own decisions. Oh, and getting paid to write about new and interesting topics each week.

And what's the worst?
Missing out on the friendships, the banter and the social interaction you get in an office environment. The anxiety when waiting for feedback and the rage if asked to make changes.

Sales and marketing

What sales/marketing channels do you use?
Being found in Google thanks to my blog, email and (very)

occasionally the phone.

Which works best for you?

My blog has helped me gain high rankings for many of my key search terms, but the most profitable assignments come from working with a marketing agency.

How do you charge for your services? By the hour/day/project/ other?

Per project. I prefer to work on something until I'm happy, rather than against the clock. I charge a set rate for articles and press releases and then per word count for other types of work. The amount can vary depending on the client and the amount of time involved.

Advice

What are the most important skills you need to be a successful freelance copywriter?

Self-discipline, a thirst for knowledge, good note taking and the ability to critique your own work. The desire to constantly improve and learn from more experienced writers.

If you were starting out again, what would you do differently (if anything)?

Approach local marketing agencies from day one, even if it meant working a couple of days a week for free.

What advice would you to give to someone considering starting out as a freelance copywriter?

Working for an agency for a few years gives you credibility, experience and a salary. I had to endure a few lean years before earning a profit. When starting out, you have the option of taking shortcuts and saying you can do something for a client and then work out how you're going to do it when you've put down the phone. But credibility and a reputation take years to build, but can be lost overnight. An ethical approach to working for clients is the best to take, both in the short and long term.

Relly Annett-Baker

http://poppycopy.co.uk

Your background

How long have you been working as a freelance copywriter?
I started in earnest around October 2007.

What were you doing before that?
I had been writing content for radio and then my husband and I started a web design agency, where I rewrote a lot of the content clients supplied us with as the English was terrible!

What was the event or motivation that led to your decision to move into freelancing?
I had a baby in June 2006 and had spent a lot of my pregnancy assuming I would be a full-time Mummy. My husband went to work for an all-star agency so we wound down the business but I realised in a few months that I was missing writing. The company my husband was working for was looking to recommend a cheap copywriter for a start-up business that needed some content, so I started doing some of the work during my baby's naptime.

What sort of business or marketing plan did you have when you started out?
That I was going to take on enough work to pay for my little boy to go to nursery for a few days a week. I was going to work for two of those days and the third I would spend baking, sewing and working on my own fiction book. In terms of marketing, I came up with a name, bought the domain, put a Wordpress

template up and got some business cards done. Then I just started telling all the people I knew in the web industry that I was available to do small bits and pieces that might not be worth sending to a copywriter otherwise. It turns out there are an awful lot of these small bits and pieces! The other thing I did plan was to go to as many local events related to the web agencies and interested parties in my area – to meet people and to explain a bit of what I did, to put on talks and workshops, and to give friends assistance with small pieces like short biographies for conferences so they could sample what I did without lumbering myself with a lot of work for gratis.

Where is your office (work at home/sublet space, etc)?

I mostly work from home, when my kids are at daycare, but I loiter anywhere with a supply of tea, wifi and a power outlet. Thankfully in Brighton we have a whole range of co-working spaces and coffee houses happy to house the wandering freelancer.

Are you a sole trader, partnership or limited company?

Currently I'm a sole trader but due to some of the larger contracts I am now being offered I might make the change to a limited company soon. Having run a company before I wouldn't recommend it until you know you need to. No-one has been bothered by my sole trader status. I think little freelance contracts are more the norm within the web industry.

Working as a freelance copywriter

Do you specialise in any industry or form of copywriting, or are you a generalist? Whichever way you work, what do you see as the advantages of that?

Yes, I do predominantly web/app based work. I'm well known for what I do and I understand my medium very well. I am lucky to work alongside some of the real movers and shakers of the web industry and have learned a lot about how a site should function and where the content fits with that. Now, everyone gets a piece of my opinion on what they are doing right or wrong!

Do you work for agencies or direct for clients or a mixture?
A mixture. In terms of copywriting, I'm quite a cheap date for web agencies pairing me up with their clients but they often get really great clients to work with so I'm happy to have a lower rate for them. I also have some long-standing contracts directly with clients.

What do see as the best thing about working as a freelance copywriter?
Gosh, what's not to like? I get to write something new every day. I wear jeans and a t-shirt to my office, in my living room. I get to give talks and workshops and show other people how to use their skills. I have some amazing clients who are genuinely changing the world as we know it. I work in a medium that is evolving and my work evolves alongside it. The fact I'm a woman has less negative impact on my working life than in practically every other arena I've worked in. Did I mention I have cookies baking in the oven as I write this?

And what's the worst?
When I get so into what I'm doing I let the cookies burn? No, seriously, as with any freelance role, it can take over your life, it can be hard to set boundaries, sometimes I procrastinate and then earn myself a whole bucket of stress, if my kids or I are sick, there isn't any backup or cover BUT I haven't done any other work that excites me so much or has given me so much creative freedom.

Sales and marketing
What sales/marketing channels do you use?
Word of mouth and recommendation. Sometimes I get inquiries through Twitter, or after speaking at conferences.

Which works best for you?

Being recommended always has the highest success rate.

How do you charge for your services? By the hour/day/project/ other?

Day rate and project rate – negotiable depending on the client and what they want to do, and the likely long-term relationship (which isn't the same as people saying 'if you do this cheaply and we launch, there might be other work in it for you...?').

Advice

What are the most important skills you need to be a successful freelance copywriter?

I'm guessing the number one answer in this survey would be 'good writing skills'. That being a given, the next important is organisation; knowing work volume and cash flow, not getting distracted by what seems urgent and putting off what actually is important. After that, a flair for self-promotion for obvious reasons.

If you were starting out again, what would you do differently (if anything)?

I'm not sure that there is. I never intended to be a 'proper' copywriter but it turns out I'm rather good at it – probably because I absorbed information about it and schooled myself knowing that I wasn't a 'proper' copywriter, that I still had a lot to learn. Maybe I'd have come up with a complete business plan and thought longer about my name and brand, but if I hadn't made it up as I went along, I'd probably never have felt ready to find a client to start with.

What advice would you to give to someone considering starting out as a freelance copywriter?

You don't need to know everything. All the fun and games of SEO, Google analytics, past historical tense, the use of definite articles in formal writing, etc., are less important than writing something, providing you are willing to learn a little bit more each day. Often my clients have shown me what I need to learn; if they are asking for details on checkout copy or on how to work in some important search terms for their market, or how best to encourage email signup from their audience, then that's what I go and research. I didn't set out with a plan. I didn't do a lot of research into 'how' to be a copywriter. I read a couple of short books on techniques and then took the plunge. I probably should have had more faith in my abilities to write at the beginning. The rest is just refinement. My first pieces stand up pretty well – they are still online in daily use and although there are tweaks I would make now, good writing is good writing.

Caroline Gibson

www.carolinegibson.co.uk

Your background

How long have you been working as a freelance copywriter?
Around 11 years.

What were you doing before that?
I worked in a number of advertising agencies. I was quite lucky to work in above-the-line and through-the-line agencies as well as branding agencies such as Wolff Olins so I managed to accumulate quite a good breadth and depth of experience.

What was the event or motivation that led to your decision to move into freelancing?
Throughout my career I've been made redundant four times and I got quite fed up when it happened again. I also had a three-year-old, so I just thought I'd give it a go. It was also quite a good time because I'd worked on a couple of big names and had just notched up a couple of awards so I was out there on a high.

What sort of business or marketing plan did you have when you started out?

None really! I was just dipping my toe in the water. But initially I worked in agencies, covering when someone was on holiday or when there was a campaign going on, but I soon began to build up my own portfolio of clients and also because I had that branding expertise, I did quite a lot of work with design agencies who don't really have copywriters in-house.

Where is your office (work at home/sublet space, etc)?

I work from home in a dedicated room, put my feet up against the radiator and crack on with it.

Are you a sole trader, partnership or limited company?

Sole trader.

Working as a freelance copywriter

Do you specialise in any industry or form of copywriting, or are you a generalist? Whichever way you work, what do you see as the advantages of that?

I don't really specialise in anything though I do have a lot of financial experience. To be honest I work across all sectors, working on a lot of web content these days. Strangely, I don't get offered many baby, feminine care or makeup projects. It tends to be pretty much across the board.

If you're a generalist you can accept anything you're offered and be confident you can do it. But I also think that tends to come with experience. I think you do bring a certain freshness, and it is great: you're writing one day about Botox and the next day about pensions.

Do you work for agencies or direct for clients or a mixture? If you work for agencies, what do they look for in a freelance copywriter?

171

When I started out it was a case of going in and spending a few weeks at agencies. I don't do that any more. I have a mixture now of working for agencies (from home) – and it does tend to be design agencies – but I have a lot of my own clients now and that's great as well.

What do see as the best thing about working as a freelance copywriter?
I think the flexibility is fantastic and it suits me down to the ground. I now have two children so if I want to go to a school assembly I can (but I also often work evenings and weekends). And the fact that you can do it anywhere in your own time. I find that some of my best ideas come to me when I'm sitting on the tube. With that, you have to be incredibly efficient and you have to treat it as running your own business.

And what's the worst?
It's never quite knowing what's around the corner. You also have to remain optimistic – when I first started out I found it quite hard not to think, "Have I achieved my monthly salary?" I'm lucky because I'm not on my own so there is another breadwinner, but if you are on your own, then the uncertainty can be a real pressure. And the fact that you don't have an IT man at hand – I wish I had one in my cupboard!

Sales and marketing
What sales/marketing channels do you use?
I really rely on my website. I get a lot of clients coming my way from my naturally high Google ranking. The web has changed so much for everyone. I also get a lot of repeat business.

Which works best for you?
My website.

How do you charge for your services? By the hour/day/project/ other?

I usually give an hourly rate but I always give a very detailed breakdown of the various stages involved. I charge for meetings, I charge for travel time and I also add on 10 per cent at the end to cover my time for emails and phone calls to the client. I do give a final figure too. I'll say "My hourly rate is X and I predict the total amount of hours will be Y."

Advice

What are the most important skills you need to be a successful freelance copywriter?

You need lots of enthusiasm. You need to be efficient, reliable and responsive, because usually clients want something done like there's no tomorrow. You need to be able to turn things around very quickly and really not to get distracted: you have to treat it as a job, as a career.

If you were starting out again, what would you do differently (if anything)?

I think it's the business side that's hard to get to grips with initially. You have to get a sense of smaller clients, who will take up a lot of time. You need to factor that in because they will need a lot more handholding.

What advice would you to give to someone considering starting out as a freelance copywriter?

I think you have to be very cautious. I've had my fingers burnt a couple of times early on where I let payments pile up and I've had to take a few people to court. You need to set out in detail, in an email, what the requirements are, what the costs are plus payment terms and conditions, what you're going to do, and get their agreement on that. You should always ask for details of their registered company name and address or sole trader details.

You shouldn't be afraid to ask for a deposit. I will sometimes agree to do the first stage and if they're happy with that, then I ask them to pay a deposit.

Caroline Hampstead

www.carolinehampstead.com

Your background
How long have you been working as a freelance copywriter
For about 5 years.

What were you doing before that?
I was working as a copywriter employed at above-the-line ad agencies.

What was the event or motivation that led to your decision to move into freelancing?
(SEE BELOW)

What sort of business or marketing plan did you have when you started out?
None. It wasn't a conscious career decision, I started freelancing having been made redundant.

Where is your office (work at home/sublet space, etc)?
At home.

Are you a sole trader, partnership or limited company?
Sole trader.

Working as a freelance copywriter
Do you specialise in any industry or form of copywriting, or are you a generalist? Whichever way you work, what do you see as the advantages of that?

I work across many sectors – from B2B to consumer, from IT to finance and food. I like the variety of working on different subjects and tend to apply the same principles whatever I'm working on. Clients provide me with the information or resources I need, and, particularly with IT, while I become an 'expert' on eg. endpoint security software during the project and absorb all the information I can on it, as soon as a project is over, the info is 'wiped' from my mind. However, I find clients find it difficult to understand how flexible copywriters are, they will ask you if you have worked on their particular sector in the past, and if you say 'No, I've never worked on pet insurance before', often (wrongly) question if you can do the job. In fact, I find knowing little about a subject means that I view it from the general public's point of view rather than an insider/industry one, which is often helpful when creating advertising or communications that are clear and accessible rather than impenetrable and loaded with industry jargon. Doing advertising is not the same as writing an academic paper or industry review.

Do you work for agencies or direct for clients or a mixture?
A mixture. I do more writing-based work direct for clients, such as writing newsletters or websites, and with agencies I tend to do more conceptual work/idea generation, eg. advertising creative work or name generation.

What do see as the best thing about working as a freelance copywriter?
The freedom, being my own boss and the lack of office politics.

And what's the worst?
The financial uncertainty, and when freelancing for an agency, you don't necessarily get the best briefs or get to see the work through.

Sales and marketing

What sales/marketing channels do you use?
Website and networking.

Which works best for you?
At the moment networking, however that may be because my website needs a rehaul. I'm also getting more into social media.

How do you charge for your services? By the hour/day/project/ other?
I prefer to charge by the hour/day, however many clients prefer to have a project fee. I've found that with project estimates I often underestimate the time they will take, especially with things like research, and end up charging too little.

Advice

What are the most important skills you need to be a successful freelance copywriter?
Apart from copywriting skills, it's useful to have good sales and negotiation skills and networking skills so that you are able to sell yourself.

If you were starting out again, what would you do differently (if anything)?
Take sales and marketing more seriously, and negotiate better.

What advice would you to give to someone considering starting out as a freelance copywriter?
Don't give up the day job until you've organised your sales and marketing and lined up some potential clients. And charge according to each job and your value to the client – it may be that working directly for a large corporate, you may be able to charge more than freelancing for an agency.

Richard Harrison
www.richwords.co.uk

Your background
How long have you been working as a freelance copywriter?
10 years.

What were you doing before that?
Working as Chief Copywriter for Sony's Information Technology division (Europe). I had responsibility for all written marketing communications concerning the VAIO PC.

What was the event or motivation that led to your decision to move into freelancing?
Multiple reasons:
- I'd endured a very intensive two-years at Sony, pre- and post-launch of the VAIO, and wanted to have a different lifestyle.
- The Sony career ladder had taken me away from copywriting (which I loved) and into marcoms project management (which was good experience, but not really what I wanted to do longer term).
- One of the freelance copywriters I used/managed on Sony projects suggested I could easily become a freelancer in the Brussels/Belgian market. He was even willing to pass on the jobs he didn't want! (This wasn't a poisoned chalice – and we became firm friends.)
- I knew I could carry on doing some work for Sony (as a freelance writer) while I built up other business.
- My Mum had died recently and left me some money. This gave me the financial security I needed to take the plunge.

What sort of business or marketing plan did you have when you started out?

Other than securing the first batch of Sony work in advance of leaving, I had no business/marketing plan.

Where is your office (work at home/sublet space etc)?
I'm now sub-letting space in a local publishing company's offices. My home office is still equipped and ready to use, but I'm only there at evenings and weekends.

Having said all that, my "office" is wherever I am with my laptop PC and iPhone.

Are you a sole trader, partnership or limited company?
I was a sole trader for about 6 years, then became a limited company (on [my] accountant's advice, for tax efficiency).

Working as a freelance copywriter

Do you specialise in any industry or form of copywriting, or are you a generalist? Whichever way you work, what do you see as the advantages of that?
My focus is the technology/consumer electronics sector, with additional key clients in business services (consultancies, trade associations, etc.) and media.

However, any freelance copywriter should be able to 'translate' their copywriting skills into multiple sectors. (My own client-base reflects this.)

Similarly, I'd say that a good writer should be able to write direct mail, press releases, brochures, web copy etc.

From a marketing perspective, however, clients seem to like specialists (e.g. DM or SEO experts) or else a sector focus (technology, for me). The advantage of either approach (or a combination) is that you can become known as one of the experts in that field, which can generate more business and allow you to charge higher fees.

Arguably, as a generalist, you'll get work from a wider range of sources. However, my experience is that it's harder to market yourself into multiple sectors/in multiple guises – and also harder to raise your rates.

Do you work for agencies or direct for clients or a mixture?
I work for communications/advertising/writing agencies from time to time, but prefer working directly with clients for two reasons: you get paid more (no agency cut or fee) and it's easier to build a relationship with the client and see opportunities for more work. Also, there's no middleman to (potentially) dilute or misunderstand the briefing/feedback.

What do you see as the best thing about working as a freelance copywriter?
Getting to do a job you enjoy, that allows you to express your creativity and use your intelligence (mostly!).

Freelance work gives you the freedom to organise your life/time the way you want to. This can bring a quality of life beyond what you can achieve on a full-time salary.

And what's the worst?
It's hard to balance working flat-out on projects with constantly marketing yourself (see below). If you don't manage this balancing act, you end up with many peaks and troughs – of work/down-time, money coming in/not coming in.

Sales and marketing
What sales/marketing channels do you use?
Face-to-face meetings with clients (used to explore their marketing needs); direct mail (including email) to generate new business and keep in touch with clients; networking (virtually, via LinkedIn etc, and in person); directory listings (like classified ads, both online and in print); my website.

Which works best for you?
Face-to-face and direct mail work best for me. I'm working on improving website traffic/traction and all forms of networking.

How do you charge for your services? By the hour/day/project/ other?
Project-by-project, but sometimes a day rate. Agencies sometimes want a quote based on an hourly rate.

Advice

What are the most important skills you need to be a successful freelance copywriter?
More than just writing skills – an understanding of marketing, sales, and psychology all feed into writing good copy and being successful in this role.

Ability to market yourself, manage your time well, maintain your motivation, negotiate with clients, take on (or delegate) the admin tasks of running a business, change according to market situation.

If you were starting out again, what would you do differently (if anything)?
Anticipating the rise/advance of the internet and social media would have provided an extremely useful competitive advantage!

What advice would you to give to someone considering starting out as a freelance copywriter?
- Use the internet to read copywriters' blogs and look at their websites.
- Get some copy training.
- Stay with your day-job until you know you've got some paying projects in the pipeline (enough for the first 3

months, ideally). In the meantime, get as much practice as you can on live projects (where possible) – perhaps by offering your services free.

- To get your first job(s), create a portfolio of ads, direct mail letters/brochures, press releases etc that you've written. Base them on real companies and their marketing collateral – perhaps simply improve what you've read on the web or in magazines/seen in shops/received through the post etc.

Anthony Hewson

www.ahcopy.co.uk

Your background

How long have you been working as a freelance copywriter?
Two years full-time now, and for a number of years previously in my spare time.

What were you doing before that?
Most recently I was a senior corporate communications and PR specialist for a FTSE 250 contractor; something I used as a stepping stone on the way to full-time writing as a career. It was an invaluable experience; a study in people, politics and big business, as well, of course, as providing a surprisingly varied amount of experience in writing, comms and PR.

What was the event or motivation that led to your decision to move into freelancing?
The comms role was always a means to an end, as I've said, but the move to freelancing as opposed to a writing role within an agency was all about timing and circumstance. Two compelling freelance opportunities arose at the same time as the end of my dealing-with-politics tether was reached…

What sort of business or marketing plan did you have when you started out?

I didn't have one. At all. The opportunities that presented themselves demanded immediate action, so I just jumped in and hoped. Planning isn't really a forte, so I have to constantly remind myself that I'm not just working, I'm running a business.

Where is your office (work at home/sublet space etc)?

My office is a bleary-eyed stumble across two treacherous stairs from the bedroom. My local coffee shop might argue that I sublet a table there too.

Are you a sole trader, partnership or limited company?

I'm a limited company – I had to be to take up my first freelance copywriting role, which was through a recruitment agency and based on client site.

Working as a freelance copywriter

Do you specialise in any industry or form of copywriting, or are you a generalist? Whichever way you work, what do you see as the advantages of that?

Because of my experience working for a major building contractor, a lot of my work is construction industry related, but I am a generalist. If I can understand a concept, a market and a need, then I can write about it. That's where research comes in. For example I knew little about the impact of art in the healing process, but now, post-article, I can hold my own in conversation on that topic. And the opportunity to tackle new topics is enormously appealing. The advantages of being a generalist are that I'm seldom bored by my work, and in theory there are more opportunities for work. The flip side is that there's more competition, it's harder to select a target to sell to, and it's harder to sell generalism – not impossible, but harder.

Do you work for agencies or direct for clients or a mixture?
It's a mixture. I try to partner with web designers, design and marketing companies and PR firms, but I also work directly with the end client.

What do see as the best thing about working as a freelance copywriter?
The best thing is the freedom from office politics – the blight of so many working lives. A close second is general freedom – I can work where and when I want, within reason and subject to deadlines!

And what's the worst?
The worst is undoubtedly not having that predictable monthly pay cheque, closely followed by the need to sell myself. I'm a reluctant salesman and a reluctant networker.

Sales and marketing

What sales/marketing channels do you use?
I have a website, of course, and a presence on the major business and social networking sites. My relationships with creative services agencies are a major sales channel and occasionally I steel myself to pick up the phone.

Which works best for you?
Agency relationships work best for me – it's the chance to work as part of a team, which as a freelancer is something to be valued.

How do you charge for your services? By the hour/day/project/ other?
I tend to charge by the hour, but establish project parameters at the outset, giving a maximum and minimum projected timescales. Provided the parameters don't change, the client knows what to expect, and nobody's being short-changed.

Advice

What are the most important skills you need to be a successful freelance copywriter?

Well, a way with words might come in handy. The ability to truly listen and to draw a brief from the most imprecise of clients. A sense of humour, an understanding of human psychology, persistence and the ability to cope with an awful lot of your own company are all pretty high on the list.

If you were starting out again, what would you do differently (if anything)?

I'd plan. Plan, plan, plan. And start selling sooner.

What advice would you to give to someone considering starting out as a freelance copywriter?

Be ready to sell – work won't always land in your in-box. You need to be ready to be your company's salesman, admin team, accounts department and more. And your own boss – try to be a strict one...

Jane Kingsmill

www.kingsmillink.com

Your background

How long have you been working as a freelance copywriter?

17 years.

What were you doing before that?

Marketing for a series of publishing companies.

What was the event or motivation that led to your decision to move into freelancing?

1) Wanting to work from home because I'd had a baby.

2) Realising that copywriting was both my favourite part of my current job and my strongest skill.

What sort of business or marketing plan did you have when you started out?
None. I just approached the companies I'd worked for previously and a few other contacts – and it went from there.

Where is your office (work at home/sublet space etc)?
In my house, although I often work in the garden when it's sunny.

Are you a sole trader, partnership or limited company?
Sole trader.

Working as a freelance copywriter

Do you specialise in any industry or form of copywriting, or are you a generalist? Whichever way you work, what do you see as the advantages of that?
I'm a generalist, although I earn most of my money from business information publishers. It depends whether you want depth or variety.

Do you work for agencies or direct for clients or a mixture?
Direct for clients until the last couple of years: I now work for a couple of agencies as well.

What do see as the best thing about working as a freelance copywriter?
Pitying the wage slaves for their Groundhog Day cycle of journey to work/boring colleagues/bad coffee/office politics/journey home, and for having to make an effort with their appearance.

And what's the worst?

Envying the wage slaves for their amusing colleagues/pub lunches/office gossip and having a steady income even when on holiday, off sick or having a nap at their desk. Oh, and for having shoes that aren't slippers.

Sales and marketing

What sales/marketing channels do you use?

My website, LinkedIn, a couple of freelance directory listings and gentle email pestering of previous, existing and potential clients.

Which works best for you?

Pestering, no question.

How do you charge for your services? By the hour/day/project/ other?

From choice, by project. But ultimately, whichever the client prefers: it works out the same anyway.

Advice

What are the most important skills you need to be a successful freelance copywriter?

Apart from actually being able to write…the ability to ask for work, be flexible over everything except quality, and keep your promises.

If you were starting out again, what would you do differently (if anything)?

I might try to find a niche like legal work, or specialise in an industry like pharmaceuticals or energy. But since I'm not trying to do it now, that's probably not true.

What advice would you to give to someone considering starting out as a freelance copywriter?

Enjoy the busy times; enjoy the quiet times.

Vince Love
http://vincelove.com

Your background

How long have you been working as a freelance copywriter?
Since 2004.

What were you doing before that?
Mostly selling, in various guises from life insurance door-to-door (20 years ago) to estate agency to businesses. I also spent some time in boutique corporate finance. I spent most time in IT – selling anything from early Macs to enterprise systems, software, network solutions and Internet/Web services.

What was the event or motivation that led to your decision to move into freelancing?
Before starting as a writer I worked mostly in sales for about 15 years and always gravitated towards writing the sales stuff that everyone else avoided. Taking product information and communicating it to an audience cogently has always given me a great sense of fulfilment and I eventually realised copywriting (or commercial writing, in the broader sense) was my vocation.

What sort of business or marketing plan did you have when you started out?
I didn't have much of one at all – certainly not a financial business plan, even though I had written quite a few before. I did quickly get my website up and running, which has been a great source of new business ever since, as well as some local marketing. Really, I just got going and took all the work I could (some of it pretty poorly paid) to sharpen my skills and build a decent portfolio.

Where is your office (work at home/sublet space, etc)?
I work from home. A home-office doesn't suit everyone but I'm

fortunate that I can balance the work/life mix even though that sometimes means I work through the night when on a roll – because I can.

Are you a sole trader, partnership or limited company?
I operate as a sole trader.

Working as a freelance copywriter

Do you specialise in any industry or form of copywriting, or are you a generalist? Whichever way you work, what do you see as the advantages of that?
I have written copy for a range of industries and will take on work whenever I honestly feel I can develop a firm grasp of the material and bring value to the client. I'm lucky that I can afford to turn down projects that don't fit with my approach or that I am not comfortable with, which happens rarely. Not unusually, I have focused more and more on eMarketing/SEO copy over the past few years mostly because I love the integration of various channels to get messages across in new and different ways to the target market. I have also written a number of eBooks on different business topics. These are the two areas I would say I specialise in, although I still produce copy in more traditional areas like brochures, ads, press releases etc. I have found that developing a reputation in a particular area causes that type of work to flow towards me more regularly; the fees are higher also.

Do you work for agencies or direct for clients or a mixture?
A real mixture. As a general rule, businesses can be more flexible and open to ideas and rely more on my advice in establishing a brief whereas agencies are more clued up and professional with a brief already defined (most of the time). Consequently, agency projects often go more smoothly (assuming the agency is experienced enough, of course) and require less client education and hand-holding.

What do see as the best thing about working as a freelance copywriter?

Independence. This has brought a number of freedoms, especially once I established my business. The obvious one is having more control of my life and future than if I was employed. But there are other advantages too, like being able to balance my business and personal life more flexibly and building more valuable relationships with clients that can be capitalised on.

And what's the worst?

To begin with, financial uncertainty, being taken advantage of by opportunistic clients and sometimes feeling quite alone in the world. Now I am established I would pretty much say there is no downside to freelance copywriting, with perhaps the occasional feeling of solitude when working days on a project without human contact.

Sales and marketing

What sales/marketing channels do you use?

My website is a great source of new business, along with referrals and some industry networking.

Which works best for you?

They are about the same. The open nature of the Web means the quality of leads from my website can vary from exceptional to absurd (I'm still surprised how many enquiries I get about services related to copyright) while referrals are more likely to result in quality projects with better fees. Of course, over time, client relationships that originate from my website mature and lead to future referrals anyway.

How do you charge for your services? By the hour/day/project/ other?

Almost always by the project. Different writers produce varying degrees of quality work at different speeds so the hourly rate can be somewhat nebulous once a project is underway. Most business clients like a fixed fee they can apply to their budgets, as do most agencies. But it's important to establish a brief in advance and be as explicit as possible about what I provide and what the client is expected to bring to the party. This methodology also enables me to schedule work more efficiently by allocating time to each project so I can manage client relationships more smoothly. This approach works for me better than charging on a time/word basis (although I do give estimates for book writing by the word). Of course, sometimes I lose out, but overall it evens out well and works for both my clients and me.

Advice

What are the most important skills you need to be a successful freelance copywriter?

- Client relationships skills – the best clients are those I work with again and again so building relationships with those clients is a large part of how I grow my business. I learn what's important about them and their market and we build a rapport over time, which results in better product. The key is about being regarded as an expert, rather than an outsourced contractor.

- Empathy – if I can walk in the audience's shoes a while I can write copy that connects with them better. I'm lucky enough to have trained as a counsellor and I use these skills often to learn about prospects (as well as the client, sometimes). Notwithstanding, remaining open and learning to feel the emotions of others, I think, is an essential skill.

- Good communications skills – I think it was Joe Baker who said, "The craft of copywriting demands an agile brain, a wide general knowledge, a high IQ and so intimate an understanding of the Queen's English that one can abuse it with impunity". I agree; technical skill of the language we write in is essential, but I always remember how important it is to write in language that will connect with the reader first.

If you were starting out again, what would you do differently (if anything)?

Work, work and get more work. I spent too much time thinking and strategising at the beginning, when trusting that I'd get better over time is what made me a better writer. And I'd work to get over perfectionism more quickly as well – it's not art, it's about selling. Much of what it takes to write good copy comes from learning the rules and techniques and using them to apply what you know about the subject – whether it be general knowledge for a slogan or researched material for Web content. Trying to produce copy worthy of awards with every word can lead to insanity, slipped deadlines and wasted time. As the saying goes – Great can be the enemy of good – especially when there is a time-sensitive business objective, which most of the time there is.

What advice would you to give to someone considering starting out as a freelance copywriter?

Learn from the masters, find others in the profession who you can connect with and don't be discouraged. It can be very tempting, especially in writing, to want to walk away because you feel like a fake or you are not good enough at the beginning. The fact is there are always clients who will value your work – you just need to find them. To begin with, seek out clients who just don't have time to write their own copy and then progress to more challenging stuff later. If there are areas you know something about then start with writing regular stuff for clients who require copy in those niches. And never forget you are in business. Setting targets and keeping to them will help maintain the discipline you need to succeed while remembering that time is your most precious resource will make you more efficient and profit-focused as you grow your business. And, of course, read lots and write a lot to improve.

Claire McCarthy

www.thetopcopy.co.uk

Your background

How long have you been working as a freelance copywriter?
Three and a half years, I started in summer 2006.

What were you doing before that?
Working full time for an academic publisher in Worcester. I worked for them for approx. four years or so, managing all of the marketing. I still help with the marketing on a freelance basis, one day a week. I'm responsible for all aspects including direct mail, the website, email marketing, and advertising, as well as those involving copywriting; this 'keeps my hand in' with marketing in general – in my opinion this is vitally important to being a successful sales copywriter. It also gives me a regular 'basic' income that I can rely on, although I supplement it significantly with freelance work.

What was the event or motivation that led to your decision to move into freelancing?
To be honest, the main motivation was moving to Bristol to live with my partner. I always wanted to move back to Bristol, where I went to university, yet loved my full-time job so much that I couldn't visualise getting another one. I enjoyed writing in particular, and decided that freelancing would suit me.

What sort of business or marketing plan did you have when you started out?
I created a simple business plan, which mainly focused on marketing and getting customers rather than the financial aspects of running a business.

For example, I had no cash flow forecast. I did spend some time researching how much I needed to charge, in order to get by, and of course I researched how to set up the business and pay taxes effectively! In retrospect I should have taken more time to research potential earnings when first starting out.

Where is your office (work at home/sublet space, etc)?
I work at home, in our 2-bedroom house. My 'office' is actually the spare room and storage dump!

Are you a sole trader, partnership or limited company?
Sole trader.

Working as a freelance copywriter

Do you specialise in any industry or form of copywriting, or are you a generalist? Whichever way you work, what do you see as the advantages of that?
I am a generalist. I don't have specific industry experience, for example medical or financial (my degree was in English & Latin). The most obvious advantage of being a generalist is having a bigger market to get work from. I know that I would also feel stifled by writing about one industry all the time – it can get repetitive.

Do you work for agencies or direct for clients or a mixture?
Mainly direct for clients. Occasionally for agencies.

What do see as the best thing about working as a freelance copywriter?
The satisfaction of completing a project, receiving positive feedback from clients and knowing that it was all my own work.

And what's the worst?
There are a couple:
- Receiving criticism, no matter how rare. Even though I always resolve the issue, I find that it knocks my confidence

and really affects my mood. I have improved over the years, but I don't have a very thick skin!

- Never being able to switch off. In the evenings or at weekends, I cannot relax as I used to – I always feel like there is something I should be doing. When I'm not working, at the back of my mind is a feeling of guilt that I never had when I worked 9 to 5 for someone else, even if I know that I am on top of my projects.

Sales and marketing

What sales/marketing channels do you use?

- A website with a regularly updated portfolio (although I am terrible at updating my own blog!). The website is SEO optimised (albeit by a complete amateur, myself).
- I am registered on plenty of free directories and freelance websites. For example FreeIndex, Google, Freelance Alliance.
- Networking – to some extent. Whilst I do not belong to a networking group such as BNI or 4Networking, when I have attended meetings as a guest I have always picked up clients, usually leading to long-term relationships and recommendations.
- Social networking. I have a Twitter account and am registered on LinkedIn. I do not use Twitter purely to 'sell', but to share and receive knowledge and experiences with fellow freelancers. Over time, I have built up some very useful relationships, which occasionally lead to new clients.

Which works best for you?

Despite my limited attendance, networking meetings have been very successful. When you get to know people, they will always turn to you first rather than someone they have never met. However, all of the other channels have brought in work for me.

How do you charge for your services? By the hour/day/project/ other?

I charge by the hour. When someone approaches me with a project, I ask questions and estimate how long it will take. I provide a maximum quote and always stick to the maximum, unless the project requirements change.

Advice

What are the most important skills you need to be a successful freelance copywriter?

- The art of persuasion. A copywriter must have an understanding of sales and marketing (at least the basics). To put it simply, copywriters should know how, and when, to sell, both in their copy, and when seeking clients!
- Organisational skills. Freelancers must be able to juggle many different projects at the same time.
- A desire and ability to learn. They must take time to learn the craft of copywriting (and keep on learning). They should read plenty of books on copywriting, sales and marketing as well as freelancing in general. They should study the techniques and read the advice of great copywriters.

If you were starting out again, what would you do differently (if anything)?

There is nothing major that I would change. However I wish I had recognised the benefits of networking sooner, it was probably a year before I attended my first networking event.

What advice would you to give to someone considering starting out as a freelance copywriter?

- Make sure it's something that you really want to do. Visit other copywriters' websites and read books on both freelancing and copywriting so that you understand what is involved. Too many people believe that good copywriting

195

is about spelling and grammar. I often use this phrase when talking about copywriting – 'It's not about knowing how to spell, it's about knowing how to sell.'

- Take time to work out how much you need to earn to get by, bearing in mind the costs of setting up a website, getting business cards, etc. You also need to be aware that you will not spend eight hours a day doing 'billable work'. You will spend a lot of time liaising with clients or potential clients, preparing quotes, networking, doing admin, etc.

- Learn about setting up a business and make sure you are aware of what is involved before you take the plunge. The Business Link website has lots of good advice.

- Don't fall into the trap of going onto auction websites, where you can 'bid' for projects. The lowest bid usually wins, and you could find yourself working for a pittance. The only exception to this advice would be if you have nothing on your portfolio and can afford to work for practically nothing while building it up.

- Put aside money for your tax every month, without fail. And be aware that when you get your very first tax bill, it will cover not only all of the tax owed for the previous tax year, but an advance payment for the first half of your next tax year!

Abbe Opher

www.writeanglecopywriting.co.uk

Your background

How long have you been working as a freelance copywriter?
I took my first copywriting job in September 2006 but I had written as a freelance journalist/features writer on and off since 2001.

What were you doing before that?
Immediately beforehand I was working as a publications officer/communications officer at an international development charity.

What was the event or motivation that led to your decision to move into freelancing?
My husband got a job 100 miles away and my employer was unhelpful in finding a viable flexible working solution. Added to which, the organisation was being restructured and my role was far less satisfactory. I was glad to make the change.

What sort of business or marketing plan did you have when you started out?
A sketchy one... although I attended Business Link courses, I was actually launching two businesses and this one didn't get as much of my attention as the other. I am now working on producing a more researched and finely tuned plan.

Where is your office (work at home/sublet space, etc)?
At home

Are you a sole trader, partnership or limited company?
Sole trader

Working as a freelance copywriter

Do you specialise in any industry or form of copywriting, or are you a generalist? Whichever way you work, what do you see as the advantages of that?
I used to work primarily for the charity sector (annual reviews, fundraising materials) but more recently I have become more of a generalist, writing marketing copy for small business people.

Do you work for agencies or direct for clients or a mixture?
Direct for clients mainly, occasionally I have been fed work from other people.

What do see as the best thing about working as a freelance copywriter?
I can fit it around the needs of my family. I don't earn a great deal but I can contribute a bit. More importantly, it gives me the chance to stay connected to my professional personality (life before children!) and interact with clients as a business woman, rather than always being a mother or a wife.

And what's the worst?
The isolation of working/wheeling and dealing alone.
But a close second is the tension that arises from my desire to do a really excellent job and the new/constant limitations on my time.

Sales and marketing

What sales/marketing channels do you use?
- Face-to-face business networking groups where I distribute business cards and flyers.
- Online business networks, forums, and job bidding sites.
- My own static website – a work in progress.

Which works best for you?
So far, face to face networking, but I'd like to attract clients by other means as this is very time consuming and relatively costly.

How do you charge for your services? By the hour/day/project/ other?
For small one-off jobs I charge by the word. Repeat/long standing clients pay an agreed set fee per project. For a large one-off project I would estimate the time required to prep and write the project.

Advice

What are the most important skills you need to be a successful freelance copywriter?

- To be able to write naturally with accuracy and insight.
- To be imaginative, perceptive and realistic so that your writing hits all the right notes with your reader.
- To be likeable – you need your client to warm to you so that you can get a good conversation going in order to get the correct type of information for a good brief.
- To be organised and focused so that you can work out a realistic deadline and write a piece that your client will be delighted with.

If you were starting out again, what would you do differently (if anything)?

I will be starting again after maternity leave so I have given this some thought – I think specialising in a sector that interests you is a very good idea. While it may seem more confined, actually you can become an expert that stands out rather than doing something that many people feel they can do. As a result you can charge more.

Linking up to marketing agencies, because getting your own work all the time is tiring, time consuming and expensive.

What advice would you to give to someone considering starting out as a freelance copywriter?

- Don't undersell yourself – there are plenty of other people on the internet who are doing that! You need to feel your writing is better, works harder and has higher integrity than the rest.
- Be pro-active about improving your writing – test yourself. That way you can be confident that you are offering an excellent service that justifies the price.
- Think about your copywriting niche. What is it?

- Don't fall into the isolation trap – get out and network. There are many different breeds of business networks from the very formal to the very chilled. Find ones where you meet people you like and can imagine working with and keep getting out of the office!

Alternatively find another way to meet people – perhaps through running workshops or writing clinics.

As soon as you stop enjoying it, stop doing it.

Sally Ormond

www.briarcopywriting.com

Your background

How long have you been working as a freelance copywriter?
My freelance copywriting career began in July 2007.

What were you doing before that?
Initially, after leaving school (with a fist of O and A Levels), I joined NatWest on their Management Development Programme. I remained there for seven years when I reached the level of Branch Manager's Assistant. I left this position to start a family and move to Suffolk (we were originally living in Northants). My first son was born in 1996 and I was happy to be a stay-at-home full-time mum. I did a lot of writing for myself at this time and self published a children's book (*The Adventures of Tilly the Tractor* and *Freddie the Fire Engine*). My second son was born in 1998.

By 2000 I was ready to get back to work and joined an international Leprosy charity working as a Community Contact Assistant on a part-time basis. Within this role I developed some regional fund-raising campaigns and wrote the direct mail letters, articles and produced the fund-raising packs (which strengthened my love and talent for writing persuasive copy).

In 2001, because being the mother of two small boys and working part-time just wasn't enough(!), I embarked on a BA (Hons) degree with the Open University in English Language and Literature. Eventually, coping with everything became too much so I resigned from my job to concentrate on my studies. In 2007 I graduated with First Class Honours. To keep my hand in the charity sector I became a volunteer Wish Granter with the Make A Wish Foundation in 2006.

What was the event or motivation that led to your decision to move into freelancing?
Once I had completed my degree I wanted to get back to work. My children were in full-time education but I wanted something with enough flexibility to enjoy a working life, but still be 'there' for them. Initially I was looking for an admin post in a school, but then something happened to change my mind.

Being self-employed wasn't something I'd really considered before. However during the final year of my degree I was studying creative writing. A good friend had volunteered to proof-read my work. Her husband had his own design agency and was also familiar with my writing. He approached me to see if I would be willing to join his team as a copywriter on a specific project they were working on. How could I refuse? It was one of those serendipitous moments which spurred me on to become a freelance copywriter (I still work with his company now).

What sort of business or marketing plan did you have when you started out?
To be honest, I didn't really have a set plan. Because I practically fell into it, it evolved organically. One thing I did know was that I had to have an online presence if I was going to make this work.

Initially I started out with a laptop and no marketing budget so I couldn't afford to get a website built. Therefore I built my own – without any HTML knowledge – that was rather a vertical learning curve!

The next step was to promote myself so I joined every online networking site I could find and started learning about social media marketing and search engine optimisation. My profile was picked up and work started coming to me. New clients came back again and again and it wasn't long before I had enough money behind me to invest in a new, professionally built website.

Because I'm not the most confident face to face networker, my main thrust was online marketing. By blogging and engaging with people on networking sites, my reputation as a copywriter soon grew as did my client base.

Where is your office (work at home/sublet space, etc)?
I work from my home office. As a mother I find this ideal as I am always around for the boys. I have a dedicated office so once the boys have left for school I can go to my desk and start the day.

Are you a sole trader, partnership or limited company?
I am a sole trader.

Working as a freelance copywriter
Do you specialise in any industry or form of copywriting, or are you a generalist? Whichever way you work, what do you see as the advantages of that?
I work as a generalist. I have written for a diverse range of industries in all sorts of formats. Although my particular skill in SEO website copywriting does mean this makes up the bulk of my work.

People have often said I should specialise but as I see it, copywriting is a skill that is easily transferable between industries and media. "Do you have experience in…" is a question I am often asked by new clients looking for someone with knowledge in a particular field. However I firmly believe that an in-depth knowledge isn't necessary in most copywriting projects (obviously if you are talking about technical reports or manuals that is a different kettle of fish). Coming into an industry without any preconceived ideas leads to copy that is fresh and vibrant – it brings something new that is eye-catching and unexpected, making it stand out from all the other messages.

This methodology has led me to work in industries as diverse as telecommunications to aesthetic cosmetic surgery and from engineering to the financial industry.

So, the way I see it, being a generalist is a great advantage to have.

Do you work for agencies or direct for clients or a mixture?
I work with a mixture. Initially I worked for individual clients or partnered up with web designers and graphic designers. However more recently I have taken on some agency work which has opened up a new world. Through the agencies I get the opportunity to work with some large blue chip companies.

This mixture therefore means my clients range from small businesses right through to large corporations.

My large online presence also means I work for companies all over the UK and abroad. Many companies in Europe approach me to help them improve and tailor their sales writing to the English market.

This mixture really helps the creativity grow. Plus it means I get to help out small businesses who really need some marketing help and work with large familiar names. I enjoy working with the 'big boys' as I still get a kick knowing that I'm working in my office at home for some of the largest names in the business world. I would like to do more work with large companies, but often find that my location in Suffolk can be off putting. Many are happy for me to work remotely, but others want me 'in-house' which in my situation simply isn't tenable.

What do see as the best thing about working as a freelance copywriter?

Apart from the obvious benefits of being your own boss and deciding which projects you want to take on and which ones you don't, I love the variety freelance copywriting brings. One day I would be working on a project for a huge corporation and the next I would be working with a one-man-band honing their marketing message.

I love the whole creative process – from collecting the brief through to thrashing out concepts and ideas to developing and refining the final message. It's a very cathartic process.

Of course, for my circumstances, being freelance is perfect. I can work when I want to, so long as all my deadlines are met. The freedom and total control are wonderful.

And what's the worst?

Definitely being Jack of all trades. I'm not only a writer, but also the Finance Director, Marketing Director, Customer Service Representative and Operations Director. Getting the balance between all of these is vital.

Taking on all of these roles also means that you can't give seven hours a day to writing for your clients – unless you are happy to do your marketing in the evening and weekends. It's all too easy to work all hours. Discipline is essential as a freelancer. Deciding on how many hours a week you'll work for clients and how much on promotion is vital if you are going to get the balance right. And no, I don't always manage to hit it right.

Understanding your own limitations and boundaries is essential. It's all too easy to take on too much. When that happens you get stressed and your marketing slips. When that slips your enquiries slip etc. It is important to make sure you put in sufficient and constant time for marketing your services to try and avoid the peaks and troughs so often associated with freelance work.

Sales and marketing

What sales/marketing channels do you use?

The vast majority of my sales/marketing is done online. Most of this is through blogging and article marketing. My blog regularly appeared in top blog lists in 2009 and to date as one of the top 11 SEO blogs in January 2010. This kind of exposure keeps my website on the front page of Google for my main keywords. But this is a constant battle so you can't let it slip.

Other than that I use Twitter a lot and have gained clients through it. I also contribute to forums when I can and use other Web 2.0 properties to build links to my main website.

Because most of my marketing has been done online, this, along with referrals, is where the vast majority of my work comes from. Last year I began to attend a few local face to face networking events. I am not the greatest networker and walking into a room of strangers fills me with dread, but the more I do it the better it gets and is also resulting in more local work.

Which works best for you?

Online networking and blogging work best for me. The success of my blog has brought me a lot of work and attention. Recently I was asked by *The Guardian* to take part in their online Q&A forum on careers in copywriting – it was only due to my online presence that I was asked to join their panel.

My blog also attracts a lot of new or prospective freelance copywriters asking for advice and guidance. I get a real buzz from talking to people about what I do and how I got started. To think that people are coming to me for advice and starting new and exciting careers in copywriting is incredible.

How do you charge for your services? By the hour/day/project/ other?

The simple answer is all of the above. The majority of my clients prefer fixed fees for projects. When pricing up a job it is vital to make sure you fully understand what is required, how many meetings your clients will want etc., to factor in all the time it will take to fulfil the brief.

However the agencies I work with prefer an hourly/daily rate. Again it is important to ensure you have full details of the project to be able to quote how many days/hours it will take if you are providing an estimate upfront.

Advice

What are the most important skills you need to be a successful freelance copywriter?

A talent for writing benefits-driven copy, a creative flair, an ability to write tight copy that is interesting, relevant and compelling.

But as well as writing you also need a determination to succeed and faith in what you do. Believe in yourself and be prepared to explain why something has been written in a certain way. Your client has hired you because you are an expert in your field, so make sure you act like one.

If you were starting out again, what would you do differently (if anything)?

I'm not sure I would do anything differently. I made the most of what I had available – which to be honest wasn't much. My lack of marketing budget made me seek out free advertising online in the shape of blogging, article marketing and networking.

Because of my circumstances and the fact that I had no contacts to tap for work I had to believe in myself. Getting online pushed me into learning about SEO which has helped me hugely with my website copywriting services – as one client put it, it's very rare to find someone who can not only write great copy, but that also understands SEO and linking structures.

My pig-headedness and desire to show everyone that I could succeed also helped. I'm not saying it was an easy ride to get where I am now. Yes, I had my doubts about whether I could pull it off and become a successful copywriter. But, nearly three years down the line, I'm still here, my client list is growing rapidly and I'm having a ball.

What advice would you to give to someone considering starting out as a freelance copywriter?
First off get as much experience as you can. If you can, start freelance in conjunction with your existing job as it can take a while before you are earning the amount you want to earn. Put your profile everywhere and start talking to people. Blog and show off your writing talents so people know you're not just full of hot air. Get yourself a good copywriting book to help you hone your talents so your writing is tight, powerful and compelling.

Start a 'swipe file' of any copy that really grabs your eye. Study it, work out what makes it good and try to emulate that in your own work.

Above all don't give up and have faith in yourself – remember freelance work can be a bit of a roller coaster ride sometimes.

Jill Tomlinson

http://jilltomlinsoncopywriting.com

Your background
How long have you been working as a freelance copywriter?
For ten years now.

What were you doing before that?
Copywriting. I was a partner in an ad agency.

What was the event or motivation that led to your decision to move into freelancing?
I was a work partner with my real-life partner and our relationship came to an end so I went freelance.

What sort of business or marketing plan did you have when you started out?

I didn't. But adrenaline makes sure you get a lot done fast!

Where is your office (work at home/sublet space, etc)?

At home.

Are you a sole trader, partnership or limited company?

I'm a limited company.

Working as a freelance copywriter

Do you specialise in any industry or form of copywriting, or are you a generalist? Whichever way you work, what do you see as the advantages of that?

I sort of do both. I do B2C accounts across a lot of general subjects – property, hotels, financials, cosmetic surgery, travel. I also do quite a lot of more specialist stuff – pharma, legal claims. I think you can write about anything if you have enough information to hand.

Do you work for agencies or direct for clients or a mixture? If you work for agencies, what do they look for in a freelance copywriter?

I do both. Agencies look for strong copywriting skills with absolute reliability, I think. Being able to work fast under pressure and being a nice person to have on the team helps a lot too. They like you even better if they trust you to interact well with their client.

What do see as the best thing about working as a freelance copywriter?

The variety of accounts. Working in an agency inevitably means your writing is restricted to a limited number of subjects. I also like the client handling aspect of freelancing. People share a lot of information about their businesses if you get the chance to spend time with them away from the keyboard. You get your own brief rather than have to interpret someone else's.

Also, the working conditions. Radio 4, the dog at my feet, a hectic schedule but one that's mine to rewrite or tear up as I please.

And what's the worst?
The awful feeling of vulnerability when something goes wrong. I have no IT department to call. IT especially is my weak point and I live in dread of something snapping, breaking, exploding into flames... Also, there are no people to chase money for me, sort my tax paperwork, bring in new business etc., etc. And there's no one to celebrate with when things go well. On the upside, I'm forced to learn about things I wouldn't go near in another life.

Sales and marketing

What sales/marketing channels do you use?
I get a lot of work from word of mouth recommendations. I now have a website too, which generates interest and I'm exploring social networking as much as time allows. If I hit quiet times though, I target agencies/clients I think are a good match and call them directly. My new year's resolution was to do this with more regularity, but, as usual, being busy gets in the way.

Which works best for you?
All approaches. If I look at my client list, they came from different sources. One really good account was a name given to me by my accountant.

How do you charge for your services? By the hour/day/project/ other?
I have an hourly rate and a day rate. More often than not I give a fixed price for a job upfront if I know pretty well how long it will take.

Advice

What are the most important skills you need to be a successful freelance copywriter?

Really good and accurate writing skills, a real interest in why people behave as they do, a sound business brain, good people skills and the ability to work well and happily under your own steam.

If you were starting out again, what would you do differently (if anything)?

I'd throw myself into learning rather than feeling anxious and under pressure, assuming you need to know everything before you start.

What advice would you to give to someone considering starting out as a freelance copywriter?

If you think you'd find it a fulfilling life, give it a real go. Just don't lose your house or your sanity in the process! An emergency fund of cash is essential during the start-up phase as, even if you're busy quickly, it takes time for money to come through. And be prepared to work hard. This is no easy option and you're unlikely to become a millionaire this way. Grafters only need apply!

Also, do it as you do your writing work ie. put the customer first. Make sure you add value for clients. Give them the kind of service they'd have to pay through the nose for if they used an agency. Then you can charge well whilst really adding bottom line benefits to businesses. Win, win.

Johnny Thomson

www.thomsonmedia.co.uk

Your background

How long have you been working as a freelance copywriter?

Since December 2001.

What were you doing before that?

I worked in the insurance industry. I was an underwriter who got into writing technical manuals (not so interesting). Project work followed, working with government departments, trade bodies etc (a bit more interesting). This led to PR/communications/ marketing work, lots of contacts (much more interesting)...

What was the event or motivation that led to your decision to move into freelancing?

Being left with no choice really. I realised several organisations wanted me to work for them, including my employer. I was lucky enough to leave my job, sign a contract with my previous employer and take up all of the other opportunities I had. A no-brainer. I probably would never have started my own business if it hadn't jumped up and slapped me in the face.

What sort of business or marketing plan did you have when you started out?

My business plan was and still is – keep it small and simple, do what I can and make the most of it while it lasts. If it doesn't work out I'll find something else to do. I'm still here.

Where is your office (work at home/sublet space etc)?

Home. Small and simple.

Are you a sole trader, partnership or limited company?

Limited company.

Working as a freelance copywriter

Do you specialise in any industry or form of copywriting, or are you a generalist? Whichever way you work, what do you see as the advantages of that?

Often insurance and related industries, health and safety, security, charities and small local firms. Frequently articles/

211

blogs for corporate communications, but I do other stuff like brochures, leaflets, websites, copylines... I like variation. Makes it more interesting.

Do you work for agencies or direct for clients or a mixture?
Almost always direct.

What do see as the best thing about working as a freelance copywriter?
The thinking time. There aren't many jobs that pay you to sit around and let your mind wander.

And what's the worst?
The work coming in waves. Lots of work/deadlines all at once, or nothing – that's often what it feels like. You get used to it though, and I've learned to enjoy the quiet times and make the most of them, knowing that it's going to get busy again.

Sales and marketing

What sales/marketing channels do you use?
Being a nice guy and doing a good job. Clients stay happy and tell others. I've got other things like a website, a blog, a flyer and I do some networking. But making people happy seems to work best.

Which works best for you?
See above.

How do you charge for your services? By the hour/day/project/ other?
Depends on the work. If an article/feature I usually charge per word. Projects, consultancy or copylines... I charge per hour.

Advice

What are the most important skills you need to be a successful freelance copywriter?

Writing! Sounds obvious, but it's a skill many people think they've got, but few actually have. An ability to explain your writing – why you've said it that way, what's the purpose, why it's going to work etc. – I find that helps a lot.

If you were starting out again, what would you do differently (if anything)?

At first I took on a lot of work from one client, leaving less time for others. I could have done it better. Eggs in one basket...

What advice would you to give to someone considering starting out as a freelance copywriter?

If you love writing – do it. If you think it's going to get you a Ferrari and a yacht on the Med to retire to – find something else to do.

Sarah Turner

www.turnerink.co.uk

Your background

How long have you been working as a freelance copywriter?

Since 2005.

What were you doing before that?

I was a marketing manager.

What was the event or motivation that led to your decision to move into freelancing?

I was made redundant and was sort of wondering what to do next. A couple of ex-colleagues started working for other

213

companies and asked if I'd come in and help put their corporate brochure and a website together. And that's how it started.

What sort of business or marketing plan did you have when you started out?
Ha ha. None at all. I still don't. I do have a To Do List. Does that count? No, seriously. I didn't have a business plan. But I very quickly worked out how many billable hours I'd have to do a day for the business to be viable.

Because I've come from an advertising and marketing background, the marketing side of the business hasn't been too difficult for me to handle. I don't have a month by month plan. But I do have a list of marketing goals.

(Reading this back it all looks a bit 'flying by the seat of my pants', doesn't it? Seems to have worked so far though!)

I've seen colleagues and friends spend weeks and weeks creating beautiful spreadsheets for their business plans but never actually getting round to doing anything about it. Sometimes I think you've just got to stop talking and go for it.

Where is your office (work at home/sublet space, etc)?
I share office space with a creative agency. I worked in a home office for a couple of years. But I actually missed the banter you get with an office environment. If I need to concentrate I just stick on my headphones and play classical music really loud. I've been much more productive since working in an office. And because the other guys here are all 'creatives' there's always people around to bounce ideas off of.

Are you a sole trader, partnership or limited company?
I'm a sole trader.

Working as a freelance copywriter

Do you specialise in any industry or form of copywriting, or are you a generalist? Whichever way you work, what do you see as the advantages of that?

Interesting question. At the beginning of my freelance copywriting career I made the decision not to have a specialist subject. I really enjoyed working for a variety of clients and didn't want to concentrate on one sector. And this still holds true today.

But I do specialise in web copy and online content

What are the advantages?

Copywriting 'gurus' state that you should be a specialist, not a generalist. And that's great if there's a sector that you love. But for me half the excitement is learning something new each week. So I'll stay a generalist for now.

Do you work for agencies or direct for clients or a mixture?

A real mixture. I work with a number of creative agencies, web designers and SEO consultants as 'their' copywriter. But I also work with clients directly who find me online or via networking.

What do see as the best thing about working as a freelance copywriter?

Working as a freelance anything is good. I'm my own boss which is a joy. Especially after some of the awful people I've worked for. And then there's the enormous sense of freedom you get from 'rowing your own boat'. You can do what you like when you want. And that's exciting. I had the romantic notion at the beginning that I'd work only a few days a week and spend the rest of the time penning my novel. Fat chance. I work longer hours now than I've ever done. But I'm not working longer hours for someone else. And that's pretty cool.

And what's the worst?

Where do I start? Late payers. Difficult clients. Lack of work. VAT returns! The money side of it can be stressful. But for the most part it's a blast.

Sales and marketing

What sales/marketing channels do you use?

I use a mixture. I network a lot. And while I've not met a huge number of direct clients this way, I've met other 'suppliers' such as web designers, PRs, and marketing consultants who I've teamed up with on various projects.

I use Social Media such as Twitter and LinkedIn. These have definitely helped me become better known in the community. And yes, I've actually got clients from Twitter.

From time to time I cold call as well. It's awful and terrifying the first time you do it. But, for the most part, people are very nice.

And I send out a monthly newsletter – without fail. This has been a fantastic way of building relationships. And it's cheap.

Which works best for you?

All of the above are important.

How do you charge for your services? By the hour/day/project/ other?

By project. I use an equation I've devised which means I can now estimate a project quite accurately. It wasn't always the case and over the years I've done a lot of 'free' work!

Advice

What are the most important skills you need to be a successful freelance copywriter?

Believe it or not, it's not writing. You can teach yourself to write. Although I guess an enthusiasm for the written word does help. This is what you need to be a freelance copywriter:

sales skills; a personality; belief in yourself; intelligence; and a massive sense of humour.

It also helps if you can touch type really fast. (I can't, but I'm getting better.)

If you were starting out again, what would you do differently (if anything)?
Ideally I would have liked to have had more cash in the bank before I started. But on the other hand the threat of starvation and eviction is a great motivator.

What advice would you to give to someone considering starting out as a freelance copywriter?
- Nick Usborne gave me this great piece of advice: don't think of yourself as being a freelance copywriter. Think of yourself as running a freelance copywriting business. There's a difference. When you're running a freelance copywriting business you need to think about sales, marketing and finance, as well as actually producing the words. I think I was about six months into my freelancing career before I realised my job was less about copywriting and more about being a salesman. (Or salesperson!)
- Immerse yourself in the copywriting community. Follow copywriters on Twitter. And read the top copywriting blogs. You'll learn tricks of the trade and you'll keep up to date with new developments in search, social media etc.
- Grab yourself some books but don't spend a fortune. Buy them second-hand on Amazon. (Note: I'm contacted about once a month by aspiring freelance copywriters. So I have a ready-made list of the top blogs to follow and the best books to buy.)
- Don't buy a database off a well known directory company. I did. In my first month. It was a total waste of money as all the information was available online for free.

- Don't fork out thousands on a swanky website when you've got nothing in your portfolio. Set up a free Wordpress blog instead. Or a page on LinkedIn so at least you have a web presence. It's free and you can use it to network.
- Get a list of all the networking groups in your area. You can normally go to one or two as a non-member. Go to all of them and then decide which group will help you grow your business. And be honest with yourself. If you're rubbish at getting up in the morning don't join a group which meets every week at 7.00am.
- Take advantage of all the free stuff on offer. The government ploughs heaps of cash into various schemes. In the beginning I went to numerous seminars run by Business Link and The Chamber of Commerce. I got a lot of 1:1 business coaching as well. And it was all free.
- Don't be frightened of the VAT office or the tax office. They're surprisingly helpful and give good advice. Remember: they want you to succeed. Otherwise you'll end up on the dole and the government will have to pay you benefits.

Peter Wise

www.ideaswise.com

Your background
How long have you been working as a freelance copywriter?
16 years.

What were you doing before that?
Full time in ad agencies.

What was the event or motivation that led to your decision to move into freelancing?
Originally, got made redundant. Found I much preferred being

my own boss and could also make more money that way.

What sort of business or marketing plan did you have when you started out?
None.

Where is your office (work at home/sublet space etc)?
Work from home or at agencies. More and more, it's from home.

Are you a sole trader, partnership or limited company?
Sole trader.

Working as a freelance copywriter

Do you specialise in any industry or form of copywriting, or are you a generalist? Whichever way you work, what do you see as the advantages of that?
Started out specialising in above the line advertising (using my previous experience) and then did a lot of direct marketing for big DM agencies. Latterly, a lot of digital, including search engine optimisation copywriting. Today I do all kinds of projects for clients all over the world, and enjoy the variety. I think the best writers can produce both good ideas and effective long copy, and what I do is a mix of that. Unlike a lot of writers, I even enjoy SEO, and advise on other aspects of this. It's gratifying to know that what you do produces concrete results – i.e. first page Google rankings.

Do you work for agencies or direct for clients or a mixture?
A mix. More and more it's clients direct, however.

What do see as the best thing about working as a freelance copywriter?
The money, the lack of office politics, the mix of work, the freedom, the creative control.

And what's the worst?
Tax returns and proofreading.

Sales and marketing

What sales/marketing channels do you use?
Apart from word of mouth, almost exclusively my own website. I've put time and effort into it and it's at or near the top of the rankings for several popular and relevant keywords. I also try and keep up with old colleagues, etc. via Linkedin and similar sites.

Which works best for you?
My website.

How do you charge for your services? By the hour/day/project/ other?
Usually by the day or half day. Occasionally by the project.

Advice

What are the most important skills you need to be a successful freelance copywriter?
Apart from the obvious language and creative skills, flexibility, curiosity, dedication, self-motivation.

If you were starting out again, what would you do differently (if anything)?
Nothing, though I'd watch out for occasional sharks and timewasters.

What advice would you to give to someone considering starting out as a freelance copywriter?
At least to start with, never turn down work if you can possibly help it. And get proofs of everything you've done, even the 'boring' bits. Somewhere, sometime, they could prove invaluable in securing you work.

PS

I hope, now that you have read this book, you have a clearer idea of both what you want to achieve as a freelance copywriter and how you're going to go about it. I won't pretend that it's an easy life – especially if that magical six-figure income appeals to you. Running a business is incredibly demanding: as you'll know by now, writing copy is the easy part. It's everything else you have to do that will keep you awake: VAT returns, tax, sales and marketing, IT, work/life balance, time management, keeping clients happy and the rest. But it is an incredibly satisfying life.

Just look at the answers our freelancers gave to question 9: what's the best thing about being a freelance copywriter? Have you ever seen so many synonyms for freedom? If I was answering that question, I'd say getting paid well to do something I love doing, for people I like, when and where I want to. As it happens I also enjoy selling and running my own business, which takes the sting out of the tail. It's true, there are quiet times, and the uncertainty about money can be worrisome. So be cautious. As soon as you can, start putting money by. Yes, buy that painting/car/gizmo you've always coveted – but remember that freelancing is often feast and famine, so stashing away as much of your surplus income as you can manage will help you feel more relaxed during lean times.

Some people go into freelancing as a gap-filler between corporate jobs. Which is fine. For me it was an irrevocable decision. If I lost the power to write I would be a gardener sooner than head back to corporate marketing. If it would have me. Which I doubt. I think you will be far more successful if you commit yourself, heart and soul, to freelancing. It can be rewarding on every level from the intellectual and financial to the personal and emotional.

Accept that you will have off days, or difficult clients, or quiet weeks … or months. Accept, too, that you will have days when you can't wait to get to your desk, when clients email you out of the blue to thank you for your work, when you get a remittance advice showing that a four-figure sum has just gone into your account, when you're home for your kids, have lunch with your spouse or get time to play sport on a weekday. There. That's why it's such a great life. So what are you waiting for? Seize the day.

About the author

Andy Maslen graduated in Psychology and Anthropology from Durham University, in England. He then started work as a sales representative for a DIY products importer. He also worked as a cook in an Italian restaurant.

In 1986, he began his marketing career, promoting business reports, journals and directories through direct mail. After ten years working in the corporate sector, including a six-year stint as a marketing director, he set up Sunfish, his copywriting agency, in 1996.

Today, he is one of the UK's leading independent copywriters, helping organisations of all sizes communicate better in writing.

Andy is a Fellow of the Institute of Direct Marketing. He writes and speaks regularly on copywriting and co-founded Write for Results, a business writing training company that numbers *The Economist* among its clients. He also publishes *Maslen on Marketing*—a free monthly e-zine.

Find out more at www.andymaslen.com